The Complete Guide to LARGE LANGUAGE MODELS (LLM)

Principles, Practice, and Deployment

By

Dr. Hesham Mohamed Elsherif

About the Author

Dr. Hesham Mohamed Elsherif stands at the forefront of library management and research, boasting an impressive 22-year tenure in the field. Holding dual doctoral degrees, one in Management and Organizational Leadership and the other in Information Systems and Technology, Dr. Elsherif brings a unique blend of knowledge to any intellectual endeavor.

An expert in Empirical research methodology, Dr. Elsherif specializes particularly in the Qualitative approach and Action research. This specialization has not only strengthened his research endeavors but has also allowed him to contribute invaluable insights and advancements in these areas.

Over the years, Dr. Elsherif has made significant contributions to the academic world not only as a professional researcher but also as an Adjunct Professor. This multifaceted role in the educational landscape has further solidified his reputation as a thought leader and pioneer.

Furthermore, Dr. Elsherif's expertise isn't confined to one region. He has served as a consultant to numerous educational institutions on an international scale, sharing best practices, innovative strategies, and his deep insights into the ever-evolving realms of management and technology.

Combining a passion for education with an unparalleled depth of knowledge, Dr. Elsherif continues to inspire, educate, and lead in both the library and academic communities.

Preface

In the era of unprecedented advances in artificial intelligence, Large Language Models (LLMs) have swiftly ascended as foundational technologies that redefine the boundaries of natural language understanding, generation, and interaction. With profound implications across education, industry, and society, the ability to build, fine-tune, and deploy these models has become an indispensable skillset for technology professionals, researchers, and decision-makers alike.

"The Complete Guide to Large Language Models: Principles, Practice, and Deployment" is specifically designed as an authoritative, yet accessible roadmap to mastering this transformative domain. Through a carefully structured approach, readers are introduced progressively from fundamental theories underpinning LLMs, including neural networks and transformer architectures, to practical applications involving pre-training, fine-tuning, and operational deployment in diverse environments.

Recognizing the complexity of translating theory into practice, this book emphasizes practical applications through comprehensive examples, step-by-step tutorials, and real-world scenarios, ensuring that readers not only understand foundational principles but also gain robust hands-on expertise. Importantly, we delve into strategies to optimize model performance, navigate resource constraints, and effectively address technical challenges encountered in real-world deployments.

Beyond the technical facets, this guide also dedicates thoughtful exploration to the ethical, legal, and societal dimensions inherent in deploying powerful LLM technologies. We underscore the responsibility that accompanies AI development, providing readers with critical insights into ethical frameworks, governance considerations, and strategies to mitigate risks, promoting conscientious and responsible innovation.

This book represents a synthesis of contemporary research, best practices, and insights drawn from industry-leading projects and pioneers in the field. Whether you are an AI practitioner aiming to sharpen your expertise, an academic pursuing deeper understanding, or a technology leader preparing your organization to strategically leverage AI capabilities, this guide equips you with the comprehensive knowledge and practical tools necessary to harness the full potential of Large Language Models.

Embark with confidence into this transformative journey through the principles, practice, and deployment of LLMs, and position yourself firmly at the vanguard of AI innovation and excellence.

Welcome to your definitive guide to mastering Large Language Models.

Table of Contents

Chapter 1: Introduction to Large Language Models (LLMs)

Definition of Large Language Models

Large Language Models (LLMs) represent a sophisticated class of artificial intelligence systems, specifically designed to comprehend, generate, and interact using natural human languages. At their core, LLMs utilize advanced neural network architectures - predominantly transformer-based structures - that enable them to process massive amounts of textual data, learning intricate patterns of syntax, semantics, and context. Unlike conventional Natural Language Processing (NLP) models, which traditionally relied heavily on human-designed linguistic rules and features, LLMs autonomously acquire their linguistic understanding through extensive training on diverse textual datasets.

Fundamentally, LLMs can be characterized by their scale and the complexity of their training procedures. The term "large" is not merely indicative of their physical size or computational resources required, but it primarily denotes the billions or even trillions of parameters these models encompass. These parameters function as adjustable variables within the neural network architecture, effectively determining the model's capability to learn, infer, and generalize linguistic patterns.

The power of LLMs lies in their versatility. They are adept at performing a multitude of language-related tasks—including text generation, question answering, summarization, translation, sentiment analysis, and even creative writing. Their capability to generalize learned knowledge and apply it across various tasks, often without significant task-specific adjustments, positions LLMs as pivotal technologies in the ongoing digital transformation of communication, automation, and intelligent decision-making.

Evolution of Large Language Models

The development and evolution of Large Language Models is marked by significant technological milestones, breakthroughs in computational power, and paradigm shifts in AI methodologies. To fully appreciate the current capabilities of LLMs, it is crucial to trace their historical trajectory and the incremental innovations that paved the way for contemporary advancements.

Early Foundations (1950s – 1980s)

Language modeling, as a concept, has its roots in early efforts to automate language translation and text-based interactions during the mid-20th century. Initial models were simplistic by today's standards, based primarily on statistical analyses and rule-based linguistic processing. During this period, NLP was dominated by symbolic approaches involving grammar and rule-based logic (e.g., Chomsky's linguistic theories), which laid important conceptual foundations but offered limited generalization and scalability.

Statistical Approaches and N-gram Models (1980s – 1990s)

In the 1980s and 1990s, language modeling underwent a pivotal shift towards statistical methods, specifically n-gram models. These models predicted the likelihood of word sequences based purely on statistical frequency data collected from large corpora. Though significantly more practical than their predecessors, n-gram models suffered from limitations in context comprehension, vocabulary coverage, and handling of long-range dependencies due to the exponential increase in data sparsity with higher-order n-grams.

Rise of Neural Networks and Word Embeddings (2000s – 2010s)

The early 2000s brought about significant innovation with the introduction of neural networks to NLP, notably with feed-forward and recurrent neural networks (RNNs). These architectures, especially RNNs and their derivatives like Long Short-Term Memory networks (LSTMs), significantly improved the modeling of context and sequence dependencies in language. Moreover, groundbreaking developments in word embeddings, such as Word2Vec, GloVe, and FastText, allowed words to be represented numerically, capturing semantic relationships between terms.

Transformers and the Birth of Modern LLMs (2017 – Present)

The true revolution in language modeling occurred with the introduction of the Transformer architecture by Vaswani et al. in 2017. Unlike RNNs, Transformers leveraged self-attention mechanisms, allowing them to handle long-range dependencies more efficiently and parallelize processing effectively. This seminal innovation drastically increased model scalability, paving the way for vastly larger and more capable models.

The subsequent release of models such as OpenAI's GPT (Generative Pre-trained Transformer) marked the onset of the "era of Large Language Models." GPT and its successors (GPT-2, GPT-3, GPT-4) demonstrated extraordinary abilities in language comprehension and generation, relying predominantly on unsupervised pre-training on massive text corpora followed by fine-tuning on specific tasks.

Notably, GPT-3, introduced by OpenAI in 2020, contained an unprecedented 175 billion parameters, effectively setting a new benchmark in model scale and capability. Its successor models and parallel efforts by other entities—such as Google's BERT, T5, and PaLM; Meta's LLaMA; and Anthropic's Claude series—further expanded and refined these capacities, integrating innovative training techniques such as reinforcement learning from human feedback (RLHF) to enhance model accuracy and alignment with human expectations.

Recent Advances and Future Trajectories

The evolution of LLMs continues at a rapid pace, driven by increasing computational resources, sophisticated training methodologies, and enhanced datasets. Recent developments include multilingual and multimodal capabilities, integration of external knowledge bases, efficient fine-tuning methods such as Low-Rank Adaptation (LoRA), and greater transparency through interpretability techniques.

Moreover, contemporary research focuses extensively on ethical implications, bias mitigation, alignment challenges, and explainability, recognizing the immense societal impact and responsibility associated with deploying such powerful technologies.

Looking forward, future iterations of LLMs are anticipated to become more computationally efficient, context-aware, interactive, and responsibly aligned with human values. As these advancements continue, Large Language Models will undoubtedly cement their role as central tools in the evolution of human-computer interaction and intelligent automation.

Significance of LLMs in Today's Technological Landscape

In the current epoch of accelerated digital transformation, Large Language Models (LLMs) have rapidly ascended as one of the most influential technological innovations, fundamentally reshaping numerous industries, academic research, communication strategies, and societal interactions. The broad applicability, unprecedented flexibility, and transformative potential of LLMs underscore their significance across diverse domains, establishing them as central pillars of contemporary technological advancements.

1. Revolutionizing Communication and Interaction

At the heart of LLMs' significance is their extraordinary capability to emulate and augment human-like communication. By understanding context, nuances, intent, and even emotional undertones, these models are fundamentally reshaping digital interactions, creating an unprecedented level of sophistication and personalization in human-computer communication.

Applications and Examples:

- **Conversational AI and Chatbots:**
  Advanced chatbots powered by LLMs, such as ChatGPT, Claude, and Bard, have dramatically improved customer service and user interactions by delivering responsive, coherent, context-aware dialogues, significantly enhancing customer satisfaction and operational efficiency.
- **Virtual Assistants and Digital Companions:**
  Technologies like Siri, Alexa, and Google Assistant have benefited substantially from LLM advancements, enabling more seamless, intuitive, and contextually aware user experiences, greatly extending their practical usability and accuracy.
- **Enhanced Human-Computer Interfaces (HCI):**
  LLMs have pushed the boundaries of traditional interfaces, promoting natural, fluid interactions across platforms—spanning text, voice, and multimodal environments—thereby democratizing access to technology and simplifying complex tasks.

2. Accelerating Innovation in Industry and Research

Large Language Models are significantly accelerating research and innovation cycles across various sectors. By synthesizing knowledge from extensive textual corpora, they facilitate rapid ideation, analysis, and knowledge generation, propelling industries into heightened states of innovation and competitiveness.

Applications and Examples:

- **Scientific Research and Discovery:**
  LLMs assist researchers in literature reviews, hypothesis generation, and data interpretation, significantly reducing research cycle times. For instance, platforms powered by LLMs enable rapid discovery of scientific insights, substantially enhancing productivity and innovation.
- **Healthcare and Biotechnology:**
  Applications such as biomedical literature analysis, drug discovery, patient assistance, and personalized medicine are dramatically benefiting from LLM-driven insights, accelerating the delivery of life-saving interventions and personalized healthcare solutions.
- **Finance and Legal Services:**
  LLMs automate extensive document analyses, risk assessments, compliance monitoring, and financial forecasting, enabling faster, data-driven decision-making, and reducing operational overhead and human error.

3. Empowering Education and Training

Education, training, and skills development have entered a transformative phase facilitated by LLM technologies. These models foster personalized learning environments, automated assessments, and interactive learning experiences, greatly enhancing educational accessibility and effectiveness.

Applications and Examples:

- **Personalized Learning Platforms:**
  Educational solutions powered by LLMs provide tailored instruction, adaptive content recommendations, and real-time feedback, significantly boosting learning outcomes and student engagement.

- **Automated Content Generation:**
  LLMs assist educators in developing high-quality teaching resources, course syllabi, and interactive educational materials efficiently, dramatically reducing workload and enhancing pedagogical quality.

- **Intelligent Tutoring Systems:**
  AI-powered tutoring systems leverage LLMs to offer individualized instruction and real-time assessment, democratizing quality education and training opportunities across diverse student populations worldwide.

4. Driving Economic Efficiency and Productivity

The integration of LLMs across various economic sectors has led to substantial efficiency gains, productivity enhancements, and competitive advantages. By automating routine cognitive tasks, optimizing workflows, and providing actionable insights, LLMs are reshaping economic productivity and operational excellence.

Applications and Examples:

- **Content Automation and Generation:**
  Businesses utilize LLM-driven tools for rapid generation of content - including marketing materials, product descriptions, technical documentation, and social media campaigns - dramatically enhancing efficiency and scale.

- **Decision Support and Analytics:**
  LLMs empower organizations to analyze large volumes of unstructured data, transforming it into actionable insights, thus facilitating informed strategic decisions and operational improvements across enterprises.

- **Enhanced Customer Experiences:**
  Companies leveraging LLM technologies for customer engagement and relationship management experience improved

response times, customer retention rates, and overall business performance.

5. Ethical Considerations and Societal Implications

The profound significance of LLMs in the modern technological landscape is further underscored by the critical ethical and societal considerations they engender. Their deployment raises essential discussions surrounding bias mitigation, transparency, accountability, and responsible AI use, shaping contemporary discourse on ethical technology deployment.

Areas of Focus:

- **Bias and Fairness:**
  LLMs trained on vast data from diverse sources inherently reflect biases present in their training corpus. Significant industry and academic efforts now prioritize bias detection, mitigation, and equitable model development to ensure fair, unbiased AI systems.
- **Transparency and Explainability:**
  Given their complexity, LLMs present challenges in transparency and interpretability. Ongoing advancements in AI explainability and interpretability frameworks are essential to foster trust, accountability, and ethical AI deployment.
- **Privacy and Security:**
  As LLMs interact intimately with sensitive data, ensuring robust privacy safeguards, compliance with data protection regulations (e.g., GDPR, CCPA), and secure deployment environments are critical considerations guiding responsible LLM utilization.

6. Strategic and Geopolitical Importance

The competitive development and deployment of Large Language Models bear strategic and geopolitical implications, becoming essential indicators of national technological advancement and capability. Nations and global corporations are increasingly prioritizing investment, research, and policy frameworks around LLMs, recognizing their strategic importance in the global technology race.

Considerations and Trends:

- **National AI Strategies:**
  Governments globally—such as the United States, China, and European Union—are integrating LLM development into national strategic priorities, recognizing their crucial role in technological leadership, economic competitiveness, and national security.
- **Technological Sovereignty:**
  Nations increasingly view LLM capabilities as essential to technological sovereignty, leading to robust investments in local research, development infrastructures, and AI talent development programs.
- **International Collaboration and Competition:**
  The global pursuit of advanced LLM capabilities has intensified both international collaboration (e.g., sharing best practices, ethical standards) and competition, reshaping technological diplomacy and international cooperation.

The extraordinary rise and extensive integration of Large Language Models into today's technological landscape represent a definitive paradigm shift in human-computer interaction, innovation, education, economic productivity, and societal dynamics. As they continue to evolve, LLMs will undoubtedly expand their impact, redefining technological possibilities and setting new standards of innovation and responsibility.

Ultimately, recognizing, understanding, and strategically leveraging the capabilities and implications of LLMs will be imperative for individuals, organizations, and societies aiming to thrive and lead within an increasingly AI-driven global environment.

Real-World Applications of Large Language Models (LLMs)

The widespread adoption and unprecedented growth of Large Language Models (LLMs) across various industries and sectors is not merely theoretical—it is deeply rooted in their extensive, diverse, and practical real-world applications. This chapter comprehensively explores the transformative use cases of LLMs, illustrating their remarkable capabilities to solve complex problems, automate intricate processes, and significantly enhance productivity, creativity, and user experiences across numerous domains.

1. Business and Customer Service

Businesses across industries leverage LLMs to enhance customer engagement, automate customer interactions, streamline internal operations, and generate insightful analytics.

Key Applications:

- **Intelligent Chatbots and Virtual Assistants**:
  Platforms like ChatGPT, Google's Bard, and Microsoft's Copilot have enabled companies to deploy sophisticated chatbots capable of handling customer queries, solving common issues, and providing detailed product information 24/7, dramatically reducing customer service costs and improving user satisfaction.
- **Automated Content Generation**:
  LLMs automate the production of marketing materials, promotional emails, product descriptions, social media content, and internal reports, significantly boosting productivity, consistency, and creativity in content marketing teams.
- **Customer Feedback Analysis**:
  LLM-driven tools analyze vast amounts of customer feedback and reviews, extracting actionable insights, sentiment analysis, and market trends, thereby helping businesses better understand their customers and improve their products and services.

2. Education and Training

LLMs have revolutionized the educational landscape by fostering personalized learning, interactive teaching, and automated content creation, significantly enhancing educational quality and accessibility.

Key Applications:

- **Personalized Learning Environments**:
  Platforms utilizing LLMs deliver personalized content tailored to individual student's needs, learning styles, and pace, greatly enhancing student engagement, motivation, and academic outcomes.

- **Automated Grading and Feedback**:
  Intelligent systems powered by LLMs efficiently grade assignments, essays, and exams, providing immediate, detailed, and personalized feedback, reducing educator workloads and allowing teachers to focus more on instructional quality.

- **Intelligent Tutoring Systems (ITS)**:
  AI-powered tutors leverage LLMs to offer highly interactive and individualized learning experiences, assisting students across subjects ranging from language learning to STEM education, democratizing high-quality education.

3. Healthcare and Life Sciences

In the healthcare sector, LLMs significantly contribute to clinical decision-making, patient communication, and biomedical research acceleration.

Key Applications:

- **Clinical Documentation and Summarization**:
  Hospitals and healthcare providers utilize LLM-based applications to automatically transcribe and summarize patient

consultations, reducing administrative workloads, minimizing errors, and improving clinical documentation accuracy.

- **Biomedical Literature Analysis**:
  Researchers employ LLMs for rapid, accurate analysis of biomedical texts, accelerating scientific discovery, identifying novel hypotheses, and synthesizing vast amounts of clinical research data effectively.
- **Patient Support and Virtual Health Assistants**:
  Virtual assistants driven by LLMs guide patients through treatment information, medication management, symptom checking, and appointment scheduling, enhancing patient engagement, adherence, and overall healthcare outcomes.

4. Finance, Banking, and Insurance

Financial institutions extensively apply LLMs for market analysis, customer engagement, compliance monitoring, and risk management.

Key Applications:

- **Financial Analysis and Forecasting**:
  LLMs rapidly process unstructured financial documents, news reports, and market data, generating insights for investment strategies, portfolio management, and economic forecasting, aiding decision-making processes.
- **Regulatory Compliance and Fraud Detection**:
  Financial organizations leverage LLM-based analytics to automate compliance monitoring, regulatory reporting, and detection of anomalies or fraudulent activities, significantly enhancing security, compliance effectiveness, and operational efficiency.
- **Customer Interaction Automation**:
  Banks and insurance companies use conversational AI systems powered by LLMs to handle customer inquiries, claims

processing, loan applications, and policy explanations, thereby improving customer experiences and operational productivity.

5. Media, Journalism, and Creative Industries

The creative industries use LLMs to streamline content production, enhance creativity, and facilitate storytelling across various digital platforms.

Key Applications:

- **Automated Journalism**:
  Media outlets such as Bloomberg and Reuters utilize LLM-driven systems to automatically generate news articles, financial summaries, sports reports, and event coverages, significantly reducing production time and cost while maintaining high content quality.
- **Scriptwriting and Creative Writing**:
  LLMs support writers and creators by generating scripts, creative storylines, dialogue suggestions, and novel literary ideas, substantially enhancing creative productivity and exploring new narrative possibilities.
- **Content Localization and Translation**:
  Media organizations leverage advanced LLMs for rapid, accurate translation and localization of content, facilitating global reach and maintaining cultural authenticity and context.

6. Legal and Regulatory Domains

LLMs are profoundly transforming legal operations, document processing, and regulatory compliance.

Key Applications:

- **Automated Legal Document Review**:
  Law firms and legal departments deploy LLMs to automate extensive reviews of contracts, case law, regulatory texts, and legal

documents, vastly improving efficiency, accuracy, and cost-effectiveness.

- **Legal Research and Case Analysis**:
  AI-driven legal research tools powered by LLMs allow lawyers and paralegals to rapidly analyze case precedents, statutes, and regulations, dramatically accelerating legal preparation and enhancing decision-making capabilities.
- **Contract Generation and Compliance Monitoring**:
  Organizations leverage LLMs for rapid generation of compliant contracts, regulatory documents, and legal reports, ensuring consistent accuracy, legal compliance, and operational agility.

7. Software Development and Technology

In the technology sector, LLMs significantly enhance developer productivity, software quality, and innovation cycles.

Key Applications:

- **AI-Assisted Coding and Development**:
  Tools such as GitHub Copilot and similar coding assistants powered by LLMs assist developers by automatically generating high-quality, optimized, and secure code snippets, dramatically improving productivity, quality, and reducing programming errors.
- **Automated Documentation and Code Summarization**:
  Software development teams employ LLMs to generate accurate technical documentation, API descriptions, and code summaries, streamlining the development lifecycle and maintaining documentation consistency.
- **Debugging and Code Review**:
  LLM-based applications identify coding errors, vulnerabilities, and potential optimizations, substantially reducing debugging

cycles, enhancing software reliability, and improving security standards.

8. Public Sector and Governance

Governments utilize LLMs for improving public services, policy analysis, citizen engagement, and administrative efficiency.

Key Applications:

- **Public Policy and Analysis**:
  Governments deploy LLM-driven analytics to rapidly process vast policy documents, public feedback, and legislative texts, generating actionable insights for policy decisions, enhancing transparency, and improving citizen engagement.
- **Citizen Engagement and Support**:
  Government agencies utilize intelligent chatbots and digital assistants powered by LLMs to provide citizens with responsive, informative assistance regarding public services, licenses, registrations, taxation, and welfare benefits.
- **Emergency Response and Crisis Management**:
  LLM systems assist public authorities by quickly analyzing large-scale crisis-related communications, social media data, and emergency information, thus improving decision-making and response effectiveness in critical situations.

9. Ethical and Social Impact Initiatives

LLMs are increasingly employed in social-good initiatives, helping address global challenges in sustainability, humanitarian aid, and accessibility.

Key Applications:

- **Climate Research and Sustainability Initiatives**:
  Organizations apply LLM-based analysis to climate and environmental literature, policy reviews, and sustainability

research, accelerating the development of impactful solutions to environmental challenges.

- **Accessibility and Inclusion**:
  Accessibility technologies leveraging LLMs support individuals with disabilities by providing intuitive, context-aware communication, inclusive digital interfaces, and personalized assistance, enhancing quality of life and societal integration.
- **Humanitarian Efforts and Disaster Response**:
  NGOs leverage LLM-driven analytics to rapidly process emergency reports, humanitarian data, and global communication streams, significantly improving disaster response, coordination efficiency, and aid effectiveness.

As illustrated comprehensively, Large Language Models have emerged as indispensable technological assets across virtually every industry and sector, profoundly reshaping modern work, education, healthcare, creativity, governance, and social initiatives. Their widespread applicability, adaptability, and transformational potential position LLMs not merely as innovative technologies but as fundamental enablers of contemporary societal and economic progress.

Through practical real-world use cases presented in this section, readers gain a deep understanding and appreciation of the diverse capabilities and critical importance of LLMs in driving technological advancement and innovation globally.

Chapter 2: Fundamental Concepts in Machine Learning

Overview of Machine Learning

Machine Learning (ML) is a subset of Artificial Intelligence (AI) focused on the development of algorithms and models that allow systems to automatically learn from data, make decisions, and improve performance over time without being explicitly programmed for specific tasks. In essence, machine learning enables computers to "learn" from examples, making it an essential component of modern AI systems, including Large Language Models (LLMs), computer vision, recommendation engines, and autonomous vehicles, among others.

The core concept behind machine learning is simple: instead of programming an explicit set of rules for a machine to follow, the system is trained on large datasets to identify patterns, relationships, and trends within that data. Over time, the model improves its ability to make predictions or decisions based on these patterns.

Machine learning algorithms are used to address a broad array of tasks across various fields, including healthcare, finance, education, marketing, and entertainment, each of which requires models capable of generalizing from past experiences to new, unseen data. This section provides an in-depth overview of the key principles, types of learning, and foundational techniques that form the basis of machine learning.

Key Principles of Machine Learning

The essence of machine learning revolves around three key principles: data, learning, and feedback. Understanding these principles provides a solid foundation for grasping the mechanisms and applications of machine learning.

1. **Data**:
   Data serves as the foundation upon which machine learning models are built. In ML, the data is typically divided into two categories:
   - **Training Data**: The dataset used to train the model. It contains labeled examples that the model uses to identify patterns.
   - **Test Data**: This data is held out during training and used to evaluate the performance of the trained model on unseen examples.
2. **Learning**:
   The process of learning involves adjusting the model's internal parameters based on the patterns observed in the training data. This is done through an optimization process where the model iteratively adjusts its parameters to reduce the error between predicted and actual outcomes.
3. **Feedback**:
   Feedback refers to the process of assessing the model's performance and fine-tuning it based on the results. In supervised learning, feedback is explicit (i.e., the true labels are provided), while in unsupervised learning, feedback is often implicit, requiring the model to find structure in the data on its own.

Types of Machine Learning

Machine learning algorithms are typically categorized into three main types based on the learning process and the nature of the data used for training:

1. Supervised Learning

Supervised learning is the most common form of machine learning and involves training a model on labeled data, where both input data and the corresponding correct outputs (labels) are provided. The goal is for the model to learn the relationship between the inputs and the correct outputs so it can predict the output for new, unseen inputs.

Key Characteristics:

- **Labeled Data**: The training data consists of input-output pairs, with the model learning to map inputs to outputs.
- **Regression and Classification**: Supervised learning tasks are typically divided into two categories:
    - **Regression**: Predicting continuous values (e.g., predicting house prices based on various features like location, size, etc.).
    - **Classification**: Predicting discrete labels or categories (e.g., identifying whether an email is spam or not).

Example Applications:

- **Spam detection** in emails
- **Medical diagnosis** (e.g., predicting whether a patient has a particular disease based on medical records)
- **Credit scoring** for loan approvals

2. Unsupervised Learning

In unsupervised learning, the model is trained on data that is not labeled. Instead of predicting a specific output, the model aims to identify hidden structures or patterns in the input data. This type of learning is used when the goal is to explore the underlying distribution of the data.

Key Characteristics:

- **Unlabeled Data**: The training data consists only of input data with no corresponding output labels.

- **Clustering and Dimensionality Reduction**: Unsupervised learning tasks often involve grouping similar data points (clustering) or reducing the number of features (dimensionality reduction) to simplify the data.

Example Applications:

- **Customer segmentation** in marketing (grouping customers by purchasing behavior)
- **Anomaly detection** (e.g., identifying unusual patterns in network traffic or financial transactions)
- **Principal Component Analysis (PCA)** for dimensionality reduction in high-dimensional data.

3. Reinforcement Learning

Reinforcement learning (RL) is a unique branch of machine learning where an agent learns by interacting with its environment and receiving feedback in the form of rewards or penalties. The agent's objective is to maximize cumulative rewards over time by learning a strategy or policy that dictates the best actions to take in various situations.

Key Characteristics:

- **Exploration and Exploitation**: The agent must balance exploring new actions and exploiting known ones to maximize rewards.
- **Trial and Error**: The agent learns through trial and error, observing the outcomes of its actions and adjusting its behavior accordingly.

Example Applications:

- **Robotics** (e.g., training a robot to navigate through a maze or pick objects)

- **Game playing** (e.g., AlphaGo or self-learning AI in video games)
- **Autonomous vehicles** (e.g., teaching a car to drive by interacting with its environment)

Basic Machine Learning Algorithms

Understanding the fundamental algorithms is essential for applying machine learning to real-world problems. Below are some of the key algorithms used in different types of machine learning.

1. Linear Regression

Linear regression is one of the simplest and most widely used algorithms for regression tasks. It models the relationship between the input features and a continuous output by fitting a straight line (or hyperplane in higher dimensions) to the data.

Mathematical Formulation:

$$y = \beta 0 + \beta 1x1 + \beta 2x2 + \cdots + \beta nXn$$

Applications:

- Predicting housing prices based on features like square footage, number of bedrooms, etc.
- Forecasting sales or financial metrics based on historical data.

2. Decision Trees

Decision trees are used for both classification and regression tasks. They split the data into subsets based on feature values and use these splits to make predictions. The resulting structure resembles a tree, where each internal node represents a decision based on a feature, and each leaf node represents a prediction.

Applications:

- Customer classification in marketing campaigns.

- Predicting loan default likelihood in finance.

3. K-Means Clustering

K-Means is one of the most popular clustering algorithms used in unsupervised learning. It divides a set of data points into K clusters based on similarity, with each point assigned to the cluster with the nearest mean.

Applications:

- Market segmentation for targeting specific customer groups.
- Image compression.

4. Neural Networks

Neural networks are a class of algorithms inspired by the human brain, consisting of layers of interconnected nodes (neurons). They are used for both supervised and unsupervised learning tasks and are particularly powerful for tasks like image and speech recognition, as well as natural language processing (NLP).

Applications:

- Image recognition (e.g., identifying objects in pictures).
- Natural Language Processing (NLP) tasks like sentiment analysis, machine translation, and text generation.

Challenges and Considerations in Machine Learning

Despite the powerful capabilities of machine learning, there are several challenges and considerations that need to be addressed in the development and deployment of ML models:

1. **Overfitting and Underfitting**:
   - **Overfitting** occurs when a model learns the training data too well, capturing noise and leading to poor generalization on new data.
   - **Underfitting** occurs when the model is too simple to capture the underlying patterns of the data.
2. **Data Quality and Quantity**:
   ML models require large amounts of high-quality data to perform well. Issues like missing data, imbalanced classes, and noisy data can severely impact model performance.
3. **Model Interpretability**:
   Many ML models, particularly complex ones like deep neural networks, are considered "black boxes" due to their lack of interpretability. Understanding how a model makes decisions is critical, especially in domains like healthcare, finance, and law.
4. **Ethical Concerns**:
   The use of machine learning raises important ethical considerations, including bias in models, fairness, transparency, and the potential for discrimination in decision-making processes.

Machine learning serves as the backbone of modern AI technologies and provides solutions to an incredibly diverse range of problems across industries. By understanding the fundamental concepts, types of learning, and key algorithms, one can begin to explore the potential of machine learning in both theoretical and practical contexts.

Neural Networks Basics

Neural Networks (NNs) represent one of the most influential and powerful paradigms in machine learning, particularly within the realm of deep learning. Neural networks are inspired by the structure and functioning of the human brain, where interconnected neurons process information through layers, making them capable of learning from data, identifying complex patterns, and making predictions. These models have become the cornerstone of modern artificial intelligence applications such as image recognition, speech processing, and natural language understanding, all of which are powered by deep neural networks.

This section delves into the fundamental concepts of neural networks, explaining their architecture, key components, and operational principles. By understanding how neural networks function, readers will be well-equipped to grasp the underlying mechanics of more advanced machine learning models, including deep learning models.

1. Introduction to Neural Networks

A neural network consists of layers of nodes, or "neurons," each performing computations on input data and passing the result to the next layer. The structure of a neural network allows it to model complex relationships and patterns in data by adjusting the weights (parameters) of connections between neurons during the training process.

The simplest form of a neural network is a **Feedforward Neural Network (FNN)**, where information moves in one direction—from the input layer, through the hidden layers, and finally to the output layer. Each layer is composed of several neurons, which are connected to neurons in the adjacent layers.

2. Key Components of a Neural Network

Neural networks are composed of several key elements that work together to process data:

a) Neurons (Nodes)

Each neuron is a basic computational unit that receives inputs, processes them, and outputs a signal. In a neural network, neurons are typically represented as nodes in a graph, where the edges represent the connections between them.

- **Input Neurons**: These neurons receive the raw data.
- **Hidden Neurons**: These neurons perform calculations on the data passed through them.
- **Output Neurons**: The neurons in the output layer generate the final predictions or classifications.

Each neuron computes a weighted sum of its inputs, adds a bias term, and applies an activation function to determine its output. The output is then sent to the next layer of neurons.

b) Layers of Neural Networks

Neural networks are structured in layers. These layers include:

- **Input Layer**: This layer receives the raw data and passes it to the next layer. Each neuron in this layer represents a feature of the input data.
- **Hidden Layers**: These are intermediate layers where the actual computation occurs. The number of hidden layers and the number of neurons within each hidden layer are key parameters that influence the network's capacity to learn complex patterns. Deep neural networks (DNNs) have many hidden layers, allowing them to learn more abstract representations of data.
- **Output Layer**: The output layer produces the final results or predictions. For example, in a classification task, the output layer may have neurons corresponding to the different classes, with the neuron that produces the highest value representing the predicted class.

c) Weights and Biases

- **Weights**: Each connection between neurons has an associated weight that determines the strength of the connection. During training, the weights are adjusted to minimize the error in the model's predictions.
- **Biases**: Each neuron has an associated bias that allows the model to fit the data more flexibly. The bias is added to the weighted sum of inputs before passing the result through the activation function.

d) Activation Functions

The activation function is a critical component of each neuron that decides whether the neuron should be activated or not, based on the input it receives. It introduces non-linearity into the network, allowing it to learn and represent complex patterns.

Common activation functions include:

- **Sigmoid**: Maps input values to a range between 0 and 1.
- **ReLU (Rectified Linear Unit)**: Outputs the input directly if it is positive; otherwise, it outputs zero.
- **Tanh**: Maps input values to a range between -1 and 1.
- **Softmax**: Often used in the output layer for multi-class classification, it converts the raw output scores into probabilities.

3. How Neural Networks Work

The core operation of a neural network involves the following steps:

1. **Forward Propagation**: The input data is passed through the network, layer by layer, where each neuron processes the data and passes the result to the next layer. The final output is produced at the output layer.

Output = Activation(Weighted Sum of Inputs + Bias)

Loss Calculation: After the forward propagation, the model's output is compared to the actual target value, and the difference (called the loss or error) is calculated. The most common loss function for regression tasks is Mean Squared Error (MSE), while for classification tasks, Cross-Entropy Loss is typically used.

2. **Backpropagation**: Backpropagation is the process through which the network adjusts its weights and biases to reduce the error. This is done by computing the gradient of the loss function with respect to each weight and bias and updating them in the opposite direction of the gradient (using an optimization algorithm like gradient descent).

Weight Update = Learning Rate × Gradient of Loss

Optimization: The weight updates are performed using an optimization algorithm. The most commonly used optimization algorithm is **Gradient Descent**, which adjusts the weights incrementally to minimize the loss function. There are various versions of gradient descent, such as:

- **Batch Gradient Descent**
- **Stochastic Gradient Descent (SGD)**
- **Mini-batch Gradient Descent**

4. Types of Neural Networks

There are various types of neural networks designed to handle specific tasks, each with a unique architecture. Some popular types include:

a) Convolutional Neural Networks (CNNs)

CNNs are a specialized type of neural network used primarily for image processing, object detection, and other computer vision tasks.

They use convolutional layers, which apply filters to the input to detect spatial hierarchies, such as edges, textures, and shapes. CNNs are highly efficient for image classification tasks because they leverage local spatial patterns and reduce the number of parameters needed.

Key components of CNNs:

- **Convolutional layers**: Apply filters to detect patterns.
- **Pooling layers**: Reduce the dimensionality of the data by downsampling.
- **Fully connected layers**: Connect all neurons to the output layer.

b) Recurrent Neural Networks (RNNs)

RNNs are designed for sequential data, where the current input depends on the previous inputs. RNNs are widely used in tasks like time series prediction, speech recognition, and natural language processing (NLP). They have feedback loops, allowing them to retain information from previous time steps, which is crucial for understanding context in sequences.

However, vanilla RNNs suffer from the problem of **vanishing gradients**, making them difficult to train for long sequences. **Long Short-Term Memory (LSTM)** networks and **Gated Recurrent Units (GRUs)** are more advanced types of RNNs that address this issue.

c) Generative Adversarial Networks (GANs)

GANs consist of two neural networks—a **generator** and a **discriminator**—that work together in a competitive setting. The generator creates fake data, while the discriminator evaluates whether the data is real or fake. The two networks are trained simultaneously, with the generator improving its ability to create realistic data, and the discriminator improving its ability to distinguish between real and fake data.

GANs are popular for generating realistic images, videos, and even text.

5. Training Neural Networks

Training a neural network is a multi-step process that requires careful tuning of parameters, selection of an appropriate dataset, and choice of an optimization technique. The key components of training a neural network include:

a) **Data Preprocessing**: The input data should be cleaned, normalized, and transformed into a suitable format. This includes scaling numerical data, encoding categorical variables, and handling missing values.

b) **Model Initialization**: Neural networks often start with random weights, which are gradually adjusted during training.

c) **Training Process**: The network is trained using forward propagation, loss calculation, and backpropagation over multiple epochs (iterations over the entire training dataset).

d) **Hyperparameter Tuning**: Key parameters such as the learning rate, the number of layers, the number of neurons in each layer, and the batch size need to be fine-tuned to optimize model performance.

e) **Evaluation and Fine-Tuning**: After training, the model is evaluated on a separate test set to assess its generalization capability. Based on performance metrics, the model may be further fine-tuned to improve accuracy.

6. Common Challenges in Neural Networks

Training neural networks involves addressing several challenges, including:

- **Overfitting**: When the model performs well on training data but poorly on test data, it has overfitted. Regularization techniques, such as dropout or L2 regularization, are used to prevent overfitting.

- **Vanishing/Exploding Gradients**: When gradients become too small or too large during backpropagation, learning can become unstable. Techniques like batch normalization and using advanced architectures (e.g., LSTMs) can alleviate this problem.
- **Computational Complexity**: Neural networks, particularly deep networks, can require a significant amount of computational resources and time. This makes training large networks computationally expensive.

Neural networks form the backbone of many state-of-the-art AI systems. By understanding the basic principles, architecture, and training methods of neural networks, readers can appreciate the underlying mechanics of more advanced deep learning techniques. Neural networks are versatile tools that power applications ranging from computer vision and natural language processing to healthcare, finance, and robotics.

Supervised vs. Unsupervised Learning

Machine learning algorithms can broadly be categorized into two main types: **Supervised Learning** and **Unsupervised Learning**. Each type of learning is characterized by the way in which data is presented to the algorithm, the type of feedback it receives, and the kinds of tasks it is used for. Understanding the distinction between these two paradigms is fundamental for applying machine learning in various real-world problems.

1. Supervised Learning

Supervised learning is the most common type of machine learning, where the algorithm is trained on labeled data. In supervised learning, both the input data and the corresponding correct output (also known as the target or label) are provided. The goal of supervised learning is for the model to learn a mapping from inputs to outputs, so it can predict the correct output for new, unseen inputs.

Key Characteristics of Supervised Learning:

- **Labeled Data**: The training data consists of input-output pairs, where each input is associated with a known output (label).
- **Goal**: The model learns to predict the output for new inputs based on the patterns it discovers in the labeled training data.
- **Error Measurement**: The error between the model's predicted output and the true output is calculated, and the model is adjusted accordingly (via techniques like backpropagation, gradient descent, etc.).

Common Types of Supervised Learning:

Supervised learning tasks are generally divided into two main types: **Regression** and **Classification**.

1. **Regression**: In regression tasks, the output is a continuous variable. The model learns to predict a numerical value based on the input features.
    - **Example**: Predicting house prices based on features such as the number of bedrooms, square footage, and location.
    - **Algorithms**: Linear Regression, Decision Trees, Support Vector Machines (SVM) for Regression, Neural Networks.
2. **Classification**: In classification tasks, the output is discrete, i.e., the model assigns input data into predefined categories or classes.
    - **Example**: Email spam detection (classifying emails as "spam" or "not spam").
    - **Algorithms**: Logistic Regression, Decision Trees, K-Nearest Neighbors (KNN), Support Vector Machines (SVM) for Classification, Neural Networks.

Illustrative Example of Supervised Learning:

Consider a simple classification task, where the goal is to predict whether an email is spam or not spam based on various features (e.g., frequency of certain words, sender, subject line).

- **Training Data**: The training data includes emails labeled as spam or not spam.
- **Model Training**: The model is trained on this labeled data and learns the features that distinguish spam emails from non-spam emails.
- **Prediction**: Once trained, the model can classify new, unseen emails as spam or not spam.

Graphical Representation:

In a simple **classification** problem, imagine plotting data points in a two-dimensional space (e.g., email word frequencies). The goal of supervised learning is to draw a decision boundary that separates different classes (e.g., spam vs. non-spam).

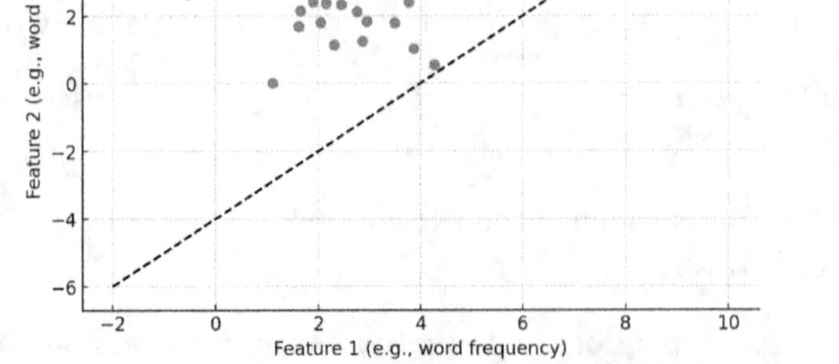

Graph: A simple linear classifier that separates spam and non-spam emails.

2. Unsupervised Learning

In contrast to supervised learning, unsupervised learning involves training the model on **unlabeled data**. The goal of unsupervised learning is to find hidden patterns, structures, or relationships in the data without any explicit guidance about the desired output. Unsupervised learning algorithms work by exploring the intrinsic structure of the data and discovering groups or representations that make sense.

Key Characteristics of Unsupervised Learning:

- **Unlabeled Data**: The training data consists of inputs without corresponding outputs. The model is not given specific labels to predict.
- **Goal**: The model aims to uncover hidden patterns or groupings in the data based on similarities or other features.
- **No Explicit Feedback**: There is no "correct answer" during training, so the model learns from the structure and distribution of the data.

Common Types of Unsupervised Learning:

Unsupervised learning tasks are generally categorized into **Clustering** and **Dimensionality Reduction**.

1. **Clustering**: The objective of clustering is to group similar data points together based on their features. The goal is to partition the dataset into distinct groups or clusters, where data points within a cluster are more similar to each other than to those in other clusters.
    - **Example**: Customer segmentation for marketing purposes, where the algorithm groups customers into different segments based on purchasing behavior.

- **Algorithms**: K-Means, DBSCAN, Agglomerative Clustering, Gaussian Mixture Models (GMM).

2. **Dimensionality Reduction**: Dimensionality reduction techniques aim to reduce the number of features (dimensions) in the data while retaining as much information as possible. These techniques help simplify the dataset, making it easier to visualize and analyze.

    - **Example**: Reducing the number of features in an image dataset to create a compressed version of the images for faster processing.

    - **Algorithms**: Principal Component Analysis (PCA), t-Distributed Stochastic Neighbor Embedding (t-SNE), Autoencoders.

Illustrative Example of Unsupervised Learning:

Consider a clustering task, where the goal is to group customers based on purchasing behavior without having any predefined labels for the groups.

- **Training Data**: The data includes features like purchase frequency, types of products bought, and average spending per visit, but no label indicating customer type.

- **Model Training**: The model uses clustering algorithms like K-Means to group customers into clusters based on similarities in their behavior.

- **Result**: The model may discover distinct customer segments such as "high spenders", "frequent buyers", and "occasional shoppers".

Graphical Representation:

In a simple **clustering** problem, imagine plotting customer data in a two-dimensional feature space. The goal of unsupervised learning is to group similar data points (customers) together based on proximity in the feature space.

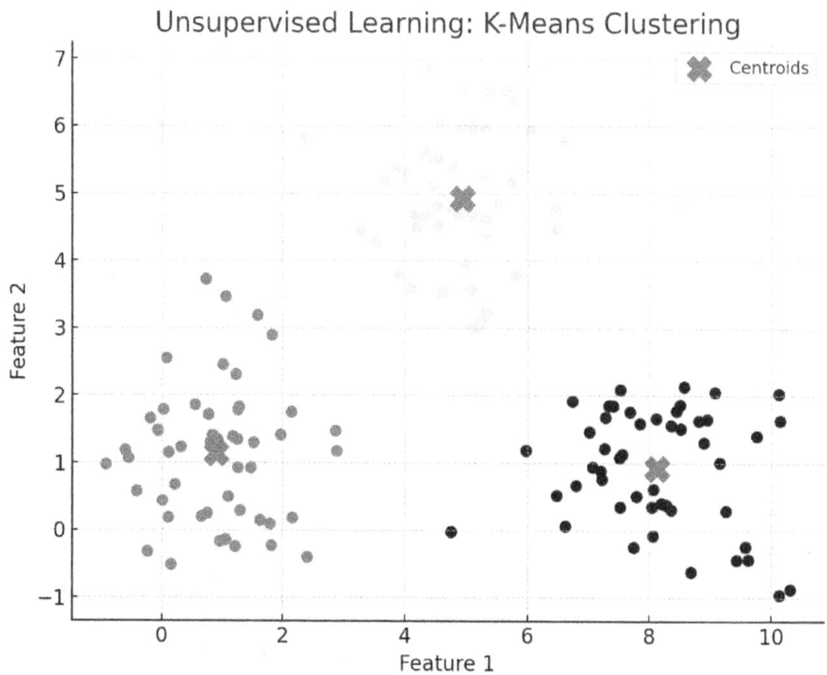

Graph: A K-Means clustering algorithm grouping data into distinct clusters.

3. Key Differences Between Supervised and Unsupervised Learning

Aspect	Supervised Learning	Unsupervised Learning
Data	Labeled data (input-output pairs).	Unlabeled data (only inputs, no explicit output).
Goal	Learn a mapping from input to output.	Discover hidden patterns or relationships in data.
Tasks	Classification, Regression.	Clustering, Dimensionality Reduction.
Examples	Spam detection, Price prediction, Medical diagnosis.	Customer segmentation, Anomaly detection, Data compression.
Feedback	Direct feedback (correct answers provided).	No direct feedback (no correct answer provided).
Model Evaluation	Evaluated based on prediction accuracy (error between prediction and actual output).	Evaluated based on how well it groups or represents the data.
Complexity	Often requires more data for accurate predictions.	Can handle raw and complex data without labeled examples.

4. Choosing Between Supervised and Unsupervised Learning

The decision to use supervised or unsupervised learning depends largely on the availability of labeled data and the problem at hand:

- **Supervised Learning** is appropriate when there is a clear relationship between input data and desired outputs, and labeled data is available. It's typically used for tasks where predictions or classifications need to be made based on historical data, such as fraud detection, stock market forecasting, and medical diagnostics.
- **Unsupervised Learning** is used when there is no labeled data available, or when the goal is to explore the data to discover patterns, trends, or groupings. It's useful for exploratory data analysis, customer segmentation, market basket analysis, and dimensionality reduction.

5. Hybrid Approaches

In practice, many machine learning systems use a combination of both supervised and unsupervised learning techniques. These hybrid approaches aim to take advantage of both the structure of labeled data and the ability to uncover patterns from unlabeled data.

For example:

- **Semi-Supervised Learning**: Uses a small amount of labeled data and a large amount of unlabeled data to train models. It is useful when labeling data is expensive or time-consuming.
- **Self-Supervised Learning**: A form of unsupervised learning where the model generates its own labels from the input data, often used in natural language processing (NLP) and computer vision.

Conclusion

Supervised and unsupervised learning are two core paradigms in machine learning, each suited to different types of problems and datasets. Understanding the differences between these approaches is essential for choosing the right technique to solve a given task. While supervised learning is ideal for tasks with labeled data where predictions or classifications are needed, unsupervised learning excels at discovering hidden structures and patterns in unlabeled data. Each approach has its strengths and weaknesses, and in many real-world applications, a combination of both is often used to achieve the best results.

Chapter 3: Understanding Natural Language Processing (NLP)

Basics of Natural Language Processing (NLP)

Natural Language Processing (NLP) is a subfield of artificial intelligence (AI) focused on the interaction between computers and human (natural) languages. The goal of NLP is to enable machines to read, understand, interpret, and generate human language in a way that is both meaningful and useful. As humans rely heavily on language for communication, NLP has become crucial in many real-world applications, ranging from virtual assistants like Siri and Alexa to advanced machine translation systems, chatbots, and sentiment analysis tools.

NLP is an interdisciplinary field that draws from linguistics, computer science, and AI. It involves various tasks such as parsing sentences, recognizing named entities, translating languages, sentiment analysis, and much more. NLP aims to process large amounts of natural language data, uncover its underlying meaning, and use it for various applications, ranging from content recommendation systems to automatic summarization and machine translation.

1. Components of Natural Language Processing

NLP can be understood through the following stages or components that form the core of the pipeline:

a) Text Preprocessing

Before a machine learning model can process natural language, the input text must undergo preprocessing. Text preprocessing involves several steps that make raw text usable for further analysis. These steps typically include:

- **Tokenization**: The process of breaking text into individual words or tokens. Tokens can also be sentences or subword units, depending on the task.

- **Lowercasing**: Converting all characters to lowercase to ensure that words like "apple" and "Apple" are treated as the same token.
- **Removing Stop Words**: Stop words are common words like "the," "and," and "in," which are typically removed because they do not carry meaningful information for many tasks.
- **Stemming**: Reducing words to their root form. For example, "running" becomes "run," and "better" becomes "good."
- **Lemmatization**: Similar to stemming, but lemmatization considers the meaning of the word and reduces it to its base or dictionary form. For instance, "ran" becomes "run" through lemmatization.

b) Syntactic Analysis (Parsing)

Syntactic analysis refers to the process of analyzing the structure of a sentence. It helps determine how words are related to each other within the sentence.

- **Part-of-Speech (POS) Tagging**: This involves assigning a grammatical label to each word in a sentence, such as noun, verb, adjective, etc. For example, in the sentence "The dog runs," "dog" is a noun and "runs" is a verb.
- **Dependency Parsing**: This identifies the relationships between words in a sentence. For example, in "The dog runs fast," the dependency parse identifies that "dog" is the subject and "runs" is the verb.
- **Constituency Parsing**: Breaks down a sentence into subcomponents, such as noun phrases and verb phrases, to identify the syntactic structure of a sentence.

c) Semantics and Meaning Representation

Once the syntax of a sentence is understood, the next step is to interpret its meaning. Semantic analysis is concerned with understanding the meaning of the text and involves tasks like:

- **Named Entity Recognition (NER)**: Identifying entities in text such as names of people, organizations, dates, or locations. For example, in the sentence "Apple Inc. was founded by Steve Jobs in Cupertino," NER identifies "Apple Inc." as an organization, "Steve Jobs" as a person, and "Cupertino" as a location.
- **Word Sense Disambiguation (WSD)**: Resolving ambiguity in words that have multiple meanings based on context. For example, the word "bank" can refer to a financial institution or the side of a river. WSD helps the model decide the correct meaning in context.
- **Coreference Resolution**: Determining which words or phrases refer to the same entity in a sentence. For example, in "John went to the store. He bought milk," coreference resolution identifies that "He" refers to "John."

d) Pragmatics

Pragmatics deals with how context influences the interpretation of meaning in natural language. It includes the study of aspects like:

- **Discourse Analysis**: Analyzing longer spans of text or conversation to understand the context and flow of information.
- **Intent Recognition**: Determining the intent behind a user's query or statement. This is especially important in conversational AI, where the goal is to understand user goals or desires from their input.

e) Language Generation

Language generation focuses on creating text that is both grammatically correct and meaningful. Some key applications include:

- **Text Generation**: Automatically generating human-like text based on a given prompt. This is used in applications like chatbots, content generation, and creative writing.
- **Machine Translation**: Automatically translating text from one language to another (e.g., Google Translate). This requires both an understanding of the syntax and semantics of the source language and the generation of grammatically correct text in the target language.
- **Summarization**: Generating a concise summary of a longer document. This can be either extractive (selecting important sentences directly from the text) or abstractive (generating new sentences that convey the main idea).

2. Core Techniques in NLP

There are several techniques used in NLP to process and represent text data. Below are some core techniques and models:

a) Bag-of-Words (BoW)

The Bag-of-Words model is one of the simplest approaches for representing text. It treats a document as a collection of words, disregarding grammar and word order, but keeping track of word frequency. Each word in the document is mapped to a unique feature in a vector space.

- **Limitations**: It does not capture word order or semantics, and the resulting vectors can be sparse when dealing with large vocabularies.

b) TF-IDF (Term Frequency-Inverse Document Frequency)

TF-IDF is an extension of the BoW model that takes into account the frequency of terms in a document and the rarity of terms across the entire corpus. It helps identify important words in a document relative to the entire dataset.

- **Formula**:

$$\text{TF-IDF}(t, d)=\text{TF}(t, d)\times\text{IDF}(t)$$

Where:

- **TF** is the term frequency of word ttt in document ddd.
- **IDF** is the inverse document frequency of word ttt across all documents.

c) Word Embeddings

Word embeddings are a more sophisticated approach to representing words. Unlike BoW and TF-IDF, word embeddings represent words as dense vectors in a continuous vector space, where semantically similar words are closer together. Common techniques include:

- **Word2Vec**: Uses a neural network to learn the vector representations of words based on their context.
- **GloVe**: Factorizes the word co-occurrence matrix into word vectors using matrix factorization techniques.
- **FastText**: Extends Word2Vec by considering subword information, allowing it to better handle rare or out-of-vocabulary words.

d) Transformers and BERT

The Transformer model, introduced by Vaswani et al. in 2017, is the foundation of modern NLP systems. It uses self-attention mechanisms to process sequences of text in parallel, rather than sequentially (as with RNNs). This allows it to capture long-range dependencies more effectively.

- **BERT (Bidirectional Encoder Representations from Transformers)**: BERT is a pre-trained transformer model that is fine-tuned for specific NLP tasks. It is bidirectional, meaning it takes context from both the left and right of a given word into account, which significantly improves its understanding of context in tasks like question answering and sentiment analysis.

3. Common NLP Tasks and Applications

NLP has a wide range of practical applications in real-world systems. Some of the most common NLP tasks include:

- **Text Classification**: Categorizing text into predefined categories. Examples include sentiment analysis (positive, negative, neutral) or topic classification (sports, politics, entertainment).
- **Named Entity Recognition (NER)**: Identifying entities such as names, locations, dates, and organizations in text.
- **Machine Translation**: Translating text from one language to another.
- **Question Answering**: Building systems that can answer questions posed in natural language based on a given text or knowledge base.
- **Speech Recognition**: Converting spoken language into text (e.g., Siri, Alexa, Google Assistant).
- **Chatbots and Conversational AI**: Building systems that can converse with humans in natural language, providing helpful responses and executing tasks.

4. Challenges in NLP

Despite significant advancements, NLP remains a challenging field due to various factors:

- **Ambiguity**: Natural language is often ambiguous, and words can have multiple meanings depending on context.
- **Contextual Understanding**: Capturing the full meaning of sentences often requires understanding the broader context, which is difficult for traditional NLP models.
- **Slang, Idioms, and Variations**: The use of slang, idiomatic expressions, and regional language variations adds complexity to NLP tasks.
- **Multilinguality**: NLP systems often struggle with languages other than English, especially when dealing with languages that have different grammatical structures, word orders, or alphabets.

Natural Language Processing (NLP) is a rapidly evolving field with vast applications in real-world systems. By combining linguistics, computer science, and machine learning, NLP enables machines to interact with human language in increasingly sophisticated ways. From basic text preprocessing and syntactic analysis to cutting-edge transformer-based models like BERT, NLP is at the forefront of enabling meaningful communication between humans and machines.

Understanding the basics of NLP, from data preprocessing to language modeling, provides a strong foundation for exploring more advanced techniques and applications. As AI continues to advance, NLP will remain a critical component of intelligent systems, enabling more natural and human-like interactions.

Tokenization and Text Preprocessing

Introduction to Tokenization and Text Preprocessing

In Natural Language Processing (NLP), **tokenization** and **text preprocessing** are crucial steps for transforming raw text data into a form that is more suitable for machine learning models. These steps ensure that the text is cleaned, standardized, and structured in a way that enables computers to effectively analyze and learn from it. Tokenization and preprocessing are the foundational stages that prepare the text for higher-level NLP tasks, such as classification, sentiment analysis, or machine translation.

1. Tokenization: Breaking Text into Meaningful Units

Tokenization is the process of dividing text into smaller, manageable pieces called **tokens**. These tokens are typically words, subwords, or sentences, depending on the granularity required for a particular task. Tokenization is an essential step because machine learning models cannot directly process raw text; they require numerical representations or organized structures of tokens to perform further analysis.

Types of Tokenization

- **Word Tokenization**: This involves splitting the text into individual words. In English, tokenization typically involves splitting on spaces, punctuation marks, or other delimiters, although more complex tokenization approaches consider special cases, such as contractions and compound words.

Example: The sentence **"I love machine learning!"** would be tokenized into the words: **["I", "love", "machine", "learning", "!"]**

- **Sentence Tokenization**: This process involves dividing the text into individual sentences. Sentence tokenization is typically more challenging than word tokenization because of punctuation marks like periods, question marks, and exclamation points, which can also appear in abbreviations or decimals.

Example: The text **"Hello there. How are you?"** would be tokenized into the sentences: **["Hello there.", "How are you?"]**

- **Subword Tokenization**: In some advanced models, such as **BERT** and **GPT**, tokenization is done at the subword level. This involves breaking down words into smaller units like prefixes, suffixes, or even individual characters, which helps handle rare words or out-of-vocabulary terms more effectively. **Byte Pair Encoding (BPE)** and **WordPiece** are popular methods for subword tokenization.

Example: The word **"unhappiness"** might be tokenized into subwords: **["un", "happiness"]**

Tokenization Example:

Consider the sentence: **"Natural language processing is exciting!"**

- **Word Tokenization**:
  ["Natural", "language", "processing", "is", "exciting", "!"]
- **Sentence Tokenization**:
  ["Natural language processing is exciting!"]
- **Subword Tokenization** (using a subword approach like BPE):
  ["Natural", "language", "pro", "cess", "ing", "is", "exciting", "!"]

2. Text Preprocessing: Preparing Text for Analysis

After tokenization, text data often requires preprocessing to clean and standardize it. Preprocessing removes noise and irrelevant information, allowing the machine learning model to focus on the relevant features of the text. The following are some key steps involved in text preprocessing:

a) Lowercasing

In NLP, it is common to convert all text to lowercase to avoid treating the same word in different cases as separate tokens. For example, "Apple" and "apple" should be treated as the same word in most text analysis tasks.

Example:

- **"I love Machine Learning!" → "i love machine learning!"**

b) Removing Punctuation and Special Characters

Punctuation marks (e.g., commas, periods, exclamation marks) and special characters often do not carry useful information for many NLP tasks, so they are usually removed. However, in certain tasks like sentiment analysis, punctuation may be important (e.g., "I love this!" vs. "I love this").

Example:

- **"I love machine learning!" → "I love machine learning"**

c) Removing Stopwords

Stopwords are common words like "the", "is", "in", and "and", which appear frequently in natural language but typically do not contribute significant meaning in many NLP tasks. Removing stopwords can help reduce the complexity of the model and improve performance.

Example:

- **"I love machine learning." → "love machine learning."**

d) Stemming

Stemming is the process of reducing words to their base or root form. The goal of stemming is to remove suffixes such as “ing”, “ed”, or “es” to group words that share a common base.

Example:

- **"running" → "run"**
- **"happier" → "happi"**

Common stemming algorithms include **Porter Stemmer** and **Snowball Stemmer**.

e) Lemmatization

Lemmatization is a more sophisticated approach to word reduction than stemming. Unlike stemming, which simply removes word endings, lemmatization uses vocabulary and grammar rules to reduce words to their base form, called the **lemma**. Lemmatization considers the meaning of the word and context, ensuring that the result is a valid word.

Example:

- **"better" → "good"**
- **"running" → "run"**

Lemmatization is often preferred in NLP tasks where the meaning of words is crucial, such as sentiment analysis.

f) Removing Numbers and Non-Alphanumeric Characters

In many text analysis tasks, numbers and non-alphanumeric characters are irrelevant and can introduce noise into the model. These are often removed unless the task specifically requires them (e.g., in financial documents, numerical data may be important).

Example:

- **"I have 2 apples." → "I have apples."**

g) Handling Negations

Negations, such as "not", "never", or "no", can alter the meaning of a sentence significantly, especially in tasks like sentiment analysis. Handling negations often involves special techniques, such as replacing "not good" with "bad" to reflect the change in sentiment.

Example:

- **"I do not like this movie." → "I dislike this movie."**

3. Example of a Full Text Preprocessing Pipeline

Let's take a sample text and walk through the steps of text preprocessing:

Original Text:
"I love Natural Language Processing, and it's amazing!"

1. **Tokenization**:
   ["I", "love", "Natural", "Language", "Processing", ",", "and", "it's", "amazing", "!"]
2. **Lowercasing**:
   ["i", "love", "natural", "language", "processing", ",", "and", "it's", "amazing", "!"]
3. **Removing Punctuation**:
   ["i", "love", "natural", "language", "processing", "and", "it's", "amazing"]
4. **Removing Stopwords**:
   ["love", "natural", "language", "processing", "amazing"]
5. **Lemmatization**:
   ["love", "natural", "language", "process", "amazing"]

6. **Final Processed Text**:
   ["love", "natural", "language", "process", "amazing"]

This processed text is now ready for further analysis, such as feature extraction or feeding into machine learning models.

4. Visualizing the Tokenization Process

To better understand tokenization, here is an illustrative graph showing how tokenization works on a sentence:

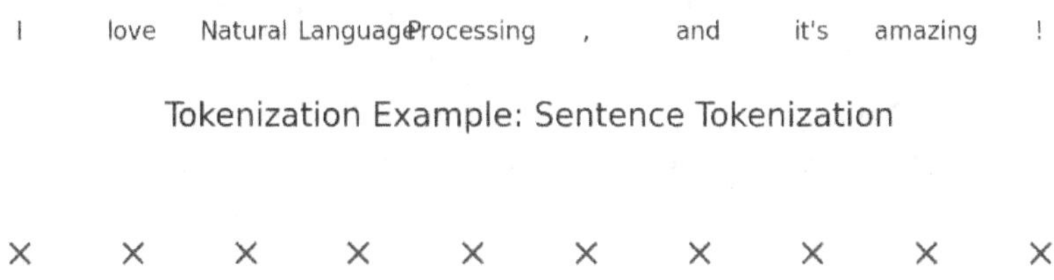

Graph: Example of sentence tokenization. Each word and punctuation mark is considered a separate token.

5. Tools and Libraries for Tokenization and Preprocessing

Several powerful libraries exist to help implement tokenization and preprocessing tasks in NLP. Some popular libraries include:

- **NLTK (Natural Language Toolkit)**: NLTK provides tools for text preprocessing, tokenization, stemming, lemmatization, and more.
- **spaCy**: spaCy is another popular library for NLP tasks that includes efficient and fast tokenization, lemmatization, and named entity recognition.
- **TextBlob**: TextBlob is an easy-to-use library that provides simple NLP operations like part-of-speech tagging, noun phrase extraction, and translation.

- **Hugging Face's Transformers**: This library offers pre-trained transformer models like BERT, GPT, and RoBERTa, which handle tokenization, feature extraction, and text classification.

Tokenization and text preprocessing are critical steps in the NLP pipeline, as they prepare raw text for analysis and ensure that the text is in a structured form that machine learning models can interpret. By tokenizing text into words or sentences and applying preprocessing techniques like lowercasing, stopword removal, and lemmatization, NLP systems can focus on the relevant information while reducing noise and complexity. With the growing demand for applications like chatbots, sentiment analysis, and machine translation, mastering these preprocessing techniques is essential for effective natural language processing.

Word Embeddings and Language Representations

In Natural Language Processing (NLP), **word embeddings** and **language representations** are pivotal concepts that enable machines to understand and process human language. These techniques transform words and phrases into numerical representations that capture the semantic meaning of words, allowing machines to perform tasks such as text classification, sentiment analysis, and machine translation with improved accuracy and efficiency.

While traditional text representations such as **Bag-of-Words (BoW)** or **Term Frequency-Inverse Document Frequency (TF-IDF)** rely on sparse vectors where each word is represented by a unique index, word embeddings and language representations offer dense, continuous vector spaces where semantically similar words are closer together. This continuous representation enables machines to understand relationships between words, their meanings, and their contexts in a way that BoW models cannot.

This section will explain the basics of word embeddings, their significance in NLP, and the various methods for generating these embeddings. It will also explore modern approaches to language representation, such as transformer models and contextualized word embeddings, which are key to achieving state-of-the-art performance in NLP.

1. Word Embeddings: Mapping Words to Vectors

Word embeddings are dense vector representations of words in a continuous vector space. The central idea behind word embeddings is that words with similar meanings should be represented by vectors that are close to each other in the vector space. These embeddings allow algorithms to process words based on their meaning, not just their syntax.

Why Use Word Embeddings?

Traditional text representation techniques like Bag-of-Words or TF-IDF often fail to capture semantic meaning. For example, in a BoW model, the words "cat" and "dog" are treated as completely different, even though they are related concepts. In contrast, word embeddings allow the model to learn that "cat" and "dog" are semantically similar because they share common features like being animals, pets, or having fur.

How Word Embeddings Work

Word embeddings map words to vectors using techniques that learn patterns from large corpora of text. These vectors are often high-dimensional, typically ranging from 50 to 300 dimensions, with each dimension capturing some aspect of the word's meaning or usage.

The most popular methods for generating word embeddings are:

1. **Word2Vec**:
   Word2Vec, introduced by Mikolov èt al. in 2013, is one of the most widely used models for generating word embeddings. Word2Vec uses a shallow neural network to predict the context words given a target word (skip-gram model) or predict the target

word given context words (Continuous Bag-of-Words (CBOW) model).

- **Skip-Gram**: The model tries to predict the surrounding context words given a central word. This approach works well for infrequent words and captures semantic meaning.
- **CBOW (Continuous Bag of Words)**: In this model, the task is to predict a target word given a surrounding context of words.

2. **GloVe (Global Vectors for Word Representation)**:
   GloVe, developed by Stanford researchers, is based on matrix factorization techniques. Instead of predicting the context of a word from a target word, GloVe captures global co-occurrence statistics of words in a corpus and uses these statistics to learn word embeddings. It aims to factorize the word co-occurrence matrix into low-dimensional vector representations.
3. **FastText**:
   FastText is an extension of Word2Vec that treats words as bags of character n-grams. This enables FastText to generate better word embeddings for rare or out-of-vocabulary words by breaking them into subword units, unlike Word2Vec, which treats words as atomic units.

Visualizing Word Embeddings

To better understand how word embeddings work, consider the following two-dimensional visualization of word embeddings using **t-SNE (t-distributed Stochastic Neighbor Embedding)**, a dimensionality reduction technique that helps visualize high-dimensional data in two dimensions:

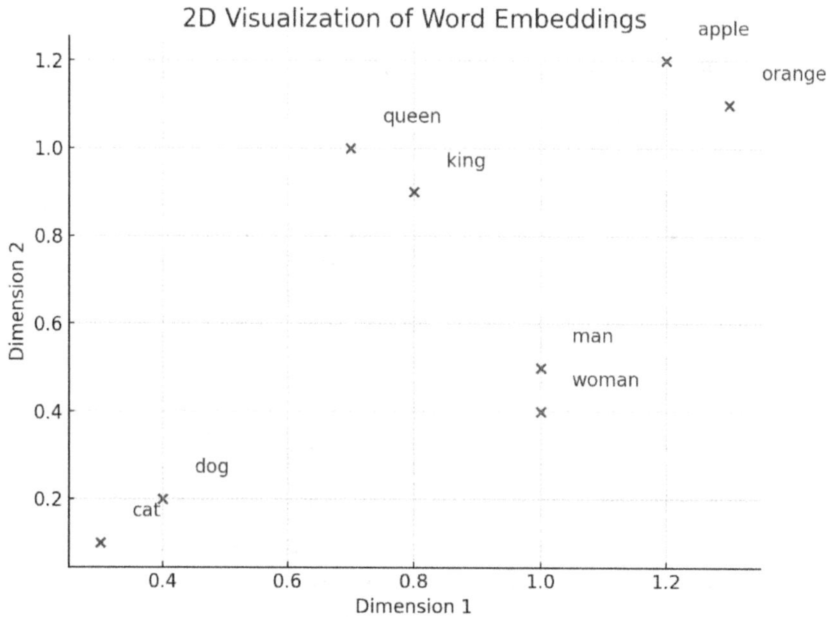

Graph: A 2D visualization of word embeddings where similar words like "king" and "queen" or "man" and "woman" are close to each other in the vector space.

This diagram shows how words with similar meanings, such as "king" and "queen", "man" and "woman", and "Paris" and "France", cluster together in the vector space.

2. Contextualized Word Embeddings: Moving Beyond Static Representations

While word embeddings like Word2Vec, GloVe, and FastText are effective, they are **static**. This means that each word has a single embedding, regardless of the context in which it appears. For example, the word **"bank"** would have the same embedding whether it refers to a **financial institution** or the **side of a river**, even though the meanings are different.

Contextualized Embeddings: The Need for Context

Contextualized word embeddings take into account the context in which a word appears, meaning that the embedding of a word can change depending on the surrounding words. This is a significant improvement over static embeddings and allows for better performance in many NLP tasks, such as question answering, machine translation, and sentiment analysis.

Transformers and BERT: Revolutionizing Word Representations

One of the most impactful innovations in NLP in recent years has been the **transformer model**, which underpins state-of-the-art models like **BERT** (Bidirectional Encoder Representations from Transformers). Transformer models can process entire sequences of text in parallel, and their attention mechanisms allow them to capture long-range dependencies in language, making them particularly powerful for generating contextualized word embeddings.

BERT and other transformer models (such as GPT, RoBERTa, and T5) represent a leap forward in language representation because they generate embeddings for words based on their surrounding context, rather than a single, static vector.

- **BERT**: BERT is pre-trained on large text corpora using the masked language model (MLM) objective, where words are randomly masked, and the model learns to predict the missing words. This pre-training enables BERT to understand word meaning based on the context provided by both preceding and following words in a sentence (bidirectional context).
- **GPT (Generative Pre-trained Transformer)**: Unlike BERT, GPT is trained using a unidirectional language model (predicting the next word given the preceding ones), but it still benefits from the transformer's attention mechanism to capture the relationships between words.

Graphical Example: BERT's Contextualized Embeddings

Consider the word **"bat"** in the following two sentences:

- **"The bat flew in the night sky."** (referring to a flying mammal)
- **"The baseball player swung the bat."** (referring to the sports equipment)

In a static embedding model like Word2Vec or GloVe, the word **"bat"** would have the same embedding in both sentences. However, in a contextualized model like BERT, the embedding of **"bat"** would differ depending on its context in each sentence, allowing the model to distinguish between the two meanings.

3. Applications of Word Embeddings and Language Representations

Word embeddings and contextualized language representations are used in a variety of NLP tasks to improve model performance and make it more scalable across different domains. Some common applications include:

a) Sentiment Analysis

Word embeddings capture semantic relationships between words, allowing models to better understand the sentiment of a text. For example, embeddings help models understand that "happy" and "joyful" convey similar sentiments, even though they are different words.

b) Named Entity Recognition (NER)

Contextual embeddings help in accurately identifying entities like names of people, organizations, or locations in a text. The model can better distinguish between **"Apple"** (the company) and **"apple"** (the fruit) based on the surrounding context.

c) Machine Translation

Word embeddings and contextualized representations are foundational to translation models, where the meaning of words must be understood in context to ensure accurate translations. Transformer-based models like **Google's Transformer** or **OpenAI's GPT** can generate more fluent and contextually accurate translations than traditional methods.

d) Question Answering Systems

Contextualized embeddings are particularly useful in question answering (QA) tasks, where a system needs to understand both the question and the context of a passage to extract the correct answer.

e) Text Generation

Language models like GPT-3 use contextualized word embeddings to generate coherent and contextually relevant text, which can be applied in applications ranging from chatbots to creative writing tools.

4. Limitations and Challenges

While word embeddings and transformer-based language models have dramatically advanced the field of NLP, they are not without their challenges:

- **Bias**: Word embeddings can inherit biases from the data they are trained on, such as gender or racial biases. For example, embeddings may associate **"doctor"** with **"male"** and **"nurse"** with **"female"**.

- **Contextual Ambiguity**: Even with contextual embeddings, models can struggle with polysemy (words with multiple meanings) or ambiguous contexts.

- **Resource-Intensive**: Training large models like BERT and GPT requires enormous computational resources, making them difficult to deploy for all users and applications.

Conclusion

Word embeddings and language representations form the backbone of modern NLP systems. By transforming words into dense, continuous vectors, and by considering the context in which words appear, these methods enable machines to understand and generate human language more effectively. From Word2Vec to BERT and GPT, advancements in word embeddings have enabled breakthroughs in NLP tasks such as sentiment analysis, machine translation, and text generation.

While these techniques have brought NLP closer to human-level language understanding, challenges such as bias and computational complexity remain. However, with continuous improvements in model architecture and training techniques, word embeddings and contextualized language representations will continue to be central to the development of more intelligent and efficient NLP systems.

Chapter 4: Deep Learning Architectures for NLP

Recurrent Neural Networks (RNNs)

Recurrent Neural Networks (RNNs) are a class of neural networks specifically designed for processing sequential data, making them highly effective for tasks involving sequences, such as text, speech, and time series data. Unlike traditional feedforward neural networks, RNNs have connections that loop back on themselves, allowing them to maintain a **memory** of previous inputs. This unique architecture makes RNNs well-suited for NLP (Natural Language Processing), where the order of words and their contextual relationships over time are crucial for understanding meaning.

RNNs have been the backbone of many foundational NLP tasks, such as machine translation, speech recognition, and language modeling, due to their ability to capture temporal dependencies and context. However, basic RNNs face limitations when dealing with long sequences, such as vanishing gradients, which hinder their ability to remember long-term dependencies.

1. Basic Architecture of Recurrent Neural Networks (RNNs)

At the core of RNNs is the **recurrent connection** between neurons. Unlike traditional feedforward neural networks where information flows in a single direction, RNNs have loops that allow information to persist, creating a form of memory.

Key Components of an RNN:

1. **Input Layer**: This layer receives the input sequence. In NLP, the input can be a sequence of words or tokens, where each word is represented as a vector (using techniques like word embeddings).
2. **Hidden Layer**: The hidden layer processes the sequence data step by step. At each time step t, the hidden state ht is updated based on both the current input xt and the previous hidden state

h_{t-1}, maintaining information about prior elements in the sequence.

- The recurrence relation at each time step is given by:

$$h_t=\sigma(W_h h_{t-1} + W_x x_t + b)$$

where W_h is the weight matrix for the hidden state, W_x is the weight matrix for the input, and σ is the activation function (typically **tanh** or **ReLU**).

3. **Output Layer**: This layer generates the output at each time step. For sequence-to-sequence tasks like language modeling or machine translation, the output is a prediction at each time step based on the current hidden state.

    - The output y_t is typically calculated as:

$$y_t = W_o h_t + b_o$$

where W_o is the weight matrix for the output, and b_o is the bias.

2. How RNNs Work: Understanding the Recurrent Nature

The key feature of RNNs is their ability to maintain information about the sequence across time steps. Here's how RNNs process a sequence of data:

a. **At each time step t**:

- The RNN receives an input x_t (e.g., a word in a sentence).
- It combines the current input x_t with the previous hidden state h_{t-1} to compute the new hidden state h_t, which contains information from both the previous time steps and the current input.
- The hidden state h_t is then passed to the next time step as well as used to generate the output y_t for the current step.

b. **Backpropagation Through Time (BPTT):**

- During training, RNNs use an extension of the standard backpropagation algorithm called **Backpropagation Through Time (BPTT)**. BPTT unrolls the RNN across the sequence and computes the gradient of the loss function with respect to each weight at every time step.
- These gradients are then used to update the model's weights.

Graphical Representation of an RNN:

Here is a simple diagram of how an RNN processes a sequence step by step:

```
              +--------------------+
x(t) --->  |  Hidden State (h(t)) | ---> y(t)
              +--------------------+
                         ^
                         |
                         |
              +--------------------+
x(t-1) ---> | Hidden State (h(t-1)) |
              +--------------------+
                         ^
                         |
                         |
              +--------------------+
x(t-2) ---> | Hidden State (h(t-2)) |
              +--------------------+
```

In the diagram:

- The input x(t) at each time step is processed along with the previous hidden state h(t−1) to generate the new hidden state h(t).

- The output y(t) is generated at each time step from the current hidden state.

3. Limitations of Basic RNNs

Despite their ability to process sequential data, **basic RNNs** suffer from a few major limitations, particularly in handling long-term dependencies in sequences. These limitations include:

a) **Vanishing Gradient Problem**: During training, as gradients are propagated back through time, they tend to shrink exponentially, especially for long sequences. This makes it difficult for basic RNNs to learn long-range dependencies effectively.

b) **Exploding Gradients**: Conversely, in some cases, gradients can grow exponentially during backpropagation, leading to numerical instability and poor convergence during training.

These issues make it challenging for basic RNNs to capture long-term dependencies and memory in sequences, such as in language tasks where earlier words in a sentence or paragraph can influence the meaning of later words.

4. Long Short-Term Memory (LSTM): Addressing RNN Limitations

To address the limitations of basic RNNs, **Long Short-Term Memory (LSTM)** networks were introduced by Hochreiter and Schmidhuber in 1997. LSTMs are a special type of RNN that includes mechanisms to better capture long-term dependencies and mitigate the vanishing gradient problem.

LSTM Architecture

LSTMs include memory cells that maintain information over long periods, as well as three key gates: the **input gate**, the **forget gate**, and the **output gate**. These gates regulate the flow of information into, out of, and within the cell, enabling LSTMs to selectively remember or forget information.

- **Input Gate**: Controls the flow of new information into the memory cell.
- **Forget Gate**: Decides what information should be discarded from the memory cell.
- **Output Gate**: Determines what part of the memory cell's state should be passed to the next time step.

These gates allow LSTMs to learn long-term dependencies by preserving useful information over time, and they significantly reduce the vanishing gradient problem.

5. Gated Recurrent Units (GRU): A Simplified LSTM

While LSTMs are effective, they are also more computationally expensive than simpler models. **Gated Recurrent Units (GRUs)**, introduced by Cho et al. in 2014, are a simpler variation of LSTMs that aim to capture long-term dependencies with fewer parameters.

Key Differences between LSTMs and GRUs:

a) **GRUs have fewer gates**: GRUs combine the input and forget gates into a single **update gate**, simplifying the architecture.

b) **GRUs share the hidden state**: In GRUs, the hidden state is updated more directly without the need for a separate cell state.

Despite being simpler, GRUs have shown comparable performance to LSTMs in many applications.

6. Applications of RNNs in NLP

RNNs and their variants (LSTMs and GRUs) are particularly well-suited for many NLP tasks due to their ability to model sequential data. Here are some common applications:

a) **Language Modeling**:

  - RNNs can be used to predict the probability of the next word in a sequence, which is the foundation of many NLP applications like autocomplete, machine translation, and text generation.

b) **Speech Recognition**:

  - RNNs process the sequential nature of speech signals to convert spoken words into text, enabling systems like Siri, Google Assistant, and Alexa.

c) **Machine Translation**:

  - RNN-based models can be used to translate text from one language to another by learning the sequence of words in the source language and predicting corresponding words in the target language.

d) **Text Summarization**:

  - RNNs can generate concise summaries of longer text documents by processing the content sequentially and outputting key points.

e) **Sentiment Analysis**:

  - RNNs are used to determine the sentiment (positive, negative, or neutral) of a given text by understanding the context of words and their relationships within a sentence.

7. Graphical Representation of LSTM and GRU

LSTM Diagram:

```
          +---------------------------+
          |                           |
ht-1 ---> |   Forget Gate             | ---> ht
          |                           |
          +---------------------------+
                        |
                        v
                +--------------+
             |  Memory Cell| <--(C_t)
                +--------------+
                        |
                        v
                +--------------+
                | Input Gate  |
                +--------------+
```

GRU Diagram:

```
ht-1 ---> [Update Gate] ----> ht
                |
                v
         +--------------+
         |  Candidate  |
         |   Hidden    |
         |    State    |
         +--------------+
```

In the diagrams:

- **LSTM** includes a memory cell and gates that control the flow of information.
- **GRU** has fewer gates but still uses mechanisms to control how information is passed through the network.

Recurrent Neural Networks (RNNs) have played a fundamental role in advancing Natural Language Processing by enabling machines to process and understand sequential data. While basic RNNs are limited by issues like vanishing gradients, more advanced architectures like LSTMs and GRUs have significantly improved the ability to capture long-range dependencies in text. These models have been widely applied in various NLP tasks, including machine translation, speech recognition, and sentiment analysis.

As NLP continues to evolve, newer architectures based on transformers, such as BERT and GPT, have further enhanced the performance of sequence-based tasks. However, RNNs, LSTMs, and GRUs remain crucial in understanding how deep learning models handle sequential data and contextual information in language tasks.

Long Short-Term Memory Networks (LSTMs)

Long Short-Term Memory (LSTM) networks are a type of **Recurrent Neural Network (RNN)** designed to address the limitations of traditional RNNs, particularly in handling long-term dependencies in sequential data. LSTMs were introduced by Hochreiter and Schmidhuber in 1997, and since then, they have become a foundational architecture for many Natural Language Processing (NLP) tasks. LSTMs are specifically designed to mitigate the **vanishing gradient problem** that traditional RNNs face when learning long-range dependencies in sequences, such as sentences, paragraphs, or entire documents.

While RNNs have the ability to process sequential data, their basic structure does not allow them to remember information over long sequences. This is particularly problematic in NLP, where the meaning of a word or phrase often depends on the context provided by earlier words. LSTMs solve this problem with a more sophisticated architecture that includes **memory cells** and **gates** that regulate the flow of information.

1. Overview of LSTM Architecture

LSTMs are a specialized type of RNN that includes a **memory cell** and three key **gates** that help control the flow of information. These gates allow the network to selectively "remember" or "forget" information as it processes sequences, enabling it to handle long-term dependencies effectively.

Key Components of LSTM Networks:

a) **Memory Cell (Cell State)**: The memory cell carries the information through the entire sequence. It acts as a "conveyor belt," passing relevant information across time steps with minimal changes, thus helping to avoid the vanishing gradient problem that affects basic RNNs.

b) **Gates**: LSTMs use three types of gates to control the flow of information:

   - **Forget Gate**: Decides which information should be discarded from the cell state. It takes the previous hidden state ht−1 and the current input xt, applies a sigmoid activation function, and outputs a value between 0 and 1, where 0 means "forget everything" and 1 means "remember everything."

   - **Input Gate**: Controls what new information should be stored in the cell state. The input gate consists of two parts: a sigmoid layer that decides which values will be updated, and a **tanh** layer that generates candidate values for updating the cell state.

   - **Output Gate**: Determines what the next hidden state should be. This hidden state contains information about the previous inputs and is passed to the next time step as well as used to generate the output.

LSTM Cell Structure:

- The forget gate controls what information to discard from the memory cell.
- The input gate decides what new information to add to the memory.
- The output gate determines what information from the memory should be output as the current hidden state.

The LSTM cell's ability to manage long-term dependencies is primarily due to these gates, which regulate the flow of information in a way that prevents the network from forgetting useful information over time.

2. Mathematical Formulation of LSTM

Let's break down the operations within the LSTM cell mathematically:

- **Forget Gate**: This gate decides which parts of the previous cell state should be forgotten:

$$f_t = \sigma(W_f[h_{t-1}, x_t] + b_f)$$

where *it* is the forget gate, σ is the sigmoid activation function, Wf is the weight matrix for the forget gate, ht−1 is the previous hidden state, and xt is the current input.

- **Input Gate**: This gate controls what new information should be stored in the cell state:

$$i_t = \sigma(W_i[h_{t-1}, x_t] + b_i)$$

$$\tilde{C}_t = \tanh(W_C[h_{t-1}, x_t] + b_C)$$

where it is the input gate, Ct is the candidate cell state, and **tanh** is the hyperbolic tangent function, which squashes the input to a range of [−1,1].

- **Cell State Update**: The cell state is updated by combining the old cell state and the new candidate cell state:

$$C_t = f_t * C_{t-1} + i_t * \tilde{C}_t$$

where Ct is the updated cell state and Ct−1 is the previous cell state.

- **Output Gate**: This gate determines the output hidden state based on the cell state and the current input:

$$o_t = \sigma(W_o[h_{t-1}, x_t] + b_o)$$

$$h_t = o_t * \tanh(C_t)$$

where ot is the output gate, and ht is the hidden state at time step t.

The combination of these gates and operations allows the LSTM to decide which information to keep and which to discard, making it effective at learning long-term dependencies in data.

3. Understanding the Memory of LSTMs

The **memory cell** is the key to LSTMs' ability to store information over long sequences. The cell state, which is updated at each time step, allows the network to retain relevant information and forget irrelevant data.

- **Forgetting Unnecessary Information**: Through the forget gate, the LSTM can "forget" certain parts of the memory that are no longer useful. For example, in long sentences, the context of earlier words may become irrelevant for later words. The forget gate helps decide when to discard such context.
- **Storing Important Information**: The input gate controls how much of the new information should be added to the cell state.

This allows the LSTM to adapt to new information while retaining past knowledge.

- **Generating Output Based on Context**: The output gate then generates the current hidden state, which is based on both the previous hidden state and the current cell state. This output contains information from both the current and past inputs, making it useful for tasks that require sequential context, such as text generation or sentiment analysis.

4. Training LSTMs: Backpropagation Through Time (BPTT)

LSTMs are trained using **Backpropagation Through Time (BPTT)**, a variant of backpropagation that unrolls the network across the entire sequence. During training, BPTT computes the gradients of the loss function with respect to the model's parameters and updates them to minimize the error.

- **Unrolling the LSTM**: BPTT involves unrolling the LSTM network over time, where each time step corresponds to a state of the LSTM network.
- **Gradient Calculation**: The gradients of the loss with respect to each weight matrix are calculated at each time step, and the parameters are updated using an optimization algorithm like **gradient descent** or its variants (e.g., **Adam optimizer**).

BPTT allows the LSTM to adjust its weights to learn the most important features from the sequence data.

5. Applications of LSTMs in NLP

LSTMs have been instrumental in advancing NLP and are widely used for various sequential tasks. Some of the most common applications of LSTMs in NLP include:

a) **Language Modeling**: LSTMs are used in language modeling to predict the probability of the next word in a sequence, which is crucial for tasks like autocomplete and speech recognition.

b) **Machine Translation**: In machine translation, LSTMs process a sequence of words in one language and generate a corresponding sequence in another language. LSTMs have been foundational in systems like Google Translate.

c) **Text Generation**: LSTMs can be used to generate coherent and contextually relevant text. They are often employed in tasks like story generation, dialogue systems, and creative writing.

d) **Speech Recognition**: LSTMs are used to recognize spoken words by processing sequential audio features and mapping them to corresponding text.

e) **Sentiment Analysis**: LSTMs are effective at analyzing sentiment in a sequence of text, allowing systems to classify text as positive, negative, or neutral based on the context of the words.

f) **Named Entity Recognition (NER)**: LSTMs are used in NER to identify entities such as people, organizations, and locations in a sequence of text. This is crucial for information extraction tasks.

g) **Text Summarization**: LSTMs help in summarizing long documents by learning to extract key information and generate concise summaries.

6. Advantages and Limitations of LSTMs

Advantages:

- **Long-Term Dependency Handling**: LSTMs are well-suited for tasks where long-term dependencies are crucial, as they can retain relevant information across long sequences.

- **Versatility**: LSTMs can handle a wide range of NLP tasks, including text generation, machine translation, and speech recognition.
- **Memory Cells**: The memory cell structure of LSTMs prevents the vanishing gradient problem, which allows them to learn over long sequences.

Limitations:

- **Computational Complexity**: LSTMs are more computationally expensive than traditional RNNs and can be slower to train due to their complex architecture.
- **Difficulty with Very Long Sequences**: Although LSTMs are designed to handle long sequences better than RNNs, they still struggle with sequences that are extremely long or require very fine-grained memory retention.
- **Requires Large Datasets**: LSTMs require large amounts of labeled data for training, especially for complex tasks like machine translation and speech recognition.

Long Short-Term Memory networks (LSTMs) have revolutionized sequential modeling in NLP by addressing the limitations of traditional RNNs and allowing models to capture long-term dependencies effectively. With their ability to remember important information and forget irrelevant data over time, LSTMs have become essential in many NLP applications, including machine translation, speech recognition, and text generation.

While newer models like transformers have surpassed LSTMs in some areas, LSTMs remain a crucial part of the NLP toolkit, particularly for sequential tasks that require careful handling of temporal relationships. As NLP continues to evolve, LSTMs will continue to serve as an important building block for many complex systems

Transformers and Attention Mechanisms

Introduction to Transformers and Attention Mechanisms

Transformers and attention mechanisms have revolutionized Natural Language Processing (NLP) by providing a more effective and scalable approach to handling sequential data compared to previous architectures such as Recurrent Neural Networks (RNNs) and Long Short-Term Memory networks (LSTMs). Introduced by Vaswani et al. in the paper *"Attention is All You Need"* in 2017, the transformer architecture quickly became the foundation for most modern NLP models, including BERT, GPT, and T5.

Transformers are designed to handle sequential data without relying on recurrent connections, instead using an innovative attention mechanism to capture dependencies across input sequences. This allows transformers to scale more efficiently and perform exceptionally well on tasks like machine translation, text generation, and question answering.

This section will provide a comprehensive explanation of transformers and attention mechanisms, detailing their architecture, how they work, and their advantages over traditional sequential models. We will also explore key transformer-based models and their applications in NLP.

1. The Transformer Architecture

The transformer architecture is based on a **self-attention mechanism**, which allows the model to weigh the importance of different words in a sequence when making predictions, regardless of their position in the sequence. Unlike RNNs or LSTMs, which process sequences step by step, transformers process the entire sequence in parallel, making them highly efficient and well-suited for long-range dependencies.

The transformer model consists of two main components:

1. **Encoder**: Processes the input sequence and generates a sequence of hidden states.
2. **Decoder**: Uses the hidden states generated by the encoder to produce the output sequence.

Both the encoder and decoder consist of multiple layers of **self-attention** and **feed-forward neural networks**.

Key Components of the Transformer Model:

1. **Self-Attention Mechanism**: The core idea behind attention is that words in a sequence do not have fixed dependencies only on adjacent words. In fact, words at the beginning of a sentence can be related to those at the end. Self-attention allows each word to focus on different words in the sequence, assigning different weights to different parts of the sentence when computing its representation.
2. **Multi-Head Attention**: Instead of having a single attention mechanism, the transformer uses **multi-head attention**, which means multiple attention mechanisms are run in parallel. This allows the model to attend to different parts of the sequence in different ways, capturing more nuanced relationships between words.
3. **Positional Encoding**: Since transformers process all words in parallel and lack a built-in mechanism for handling the order of words, they use **positional encodings** to inject information about the position of each word in the sequence. This is typically done by adding a fixed or learned vector to the word embeddings, which encodes the position of the word in the sequence.
4. **Feed-Forward Neural Networks**: After the attention mechanism, the transformer includes a feed-forward neural

network applied to each position independently. This network typically consists of two layers: a linear transformation followed by a non-linear activation function (e.g., ReLU).

5. **Layer Normalization and Residual Connections**: Each sub-layer (e.g., attention layer and feed-forward network) is followed by layer normalization and a residual connection, which helps improve training and prevent vanishing gradients.

The Transformer Encoder-Decoder Architecture:

- **Encoder**: The encoder takes the input sequence and processes it using multiple layers of self-attention and feed-forward networks. The output of the encoder is a sequence of hidden states.
- **Decoder**: The decoder uses the encoder's output and generates the final output sequence. It includes layers of self-attention, multi-head attention (which attends to the encoder's output), and feed-forward networks.

2. The Attention Mechanism

The attention mechanism is a core component of transformers, allowing them to focus on different parts of the input sequence while making predictions. Instead of processing sequences step by step, attention enables the model to look at all positions of the sequence simultaneously and decide which parts are most relevant.

Scaled Dot-Product Attention

The simplest form of attention used in transformers is **scaled dot-product attention**, which computes the attention weights based on the similarity between queries, keys, and values. Given an input sequence of words, the attention mechanism performs the following steps:

a) **Query, Key, and Value**: Each word in the sequence is represented as a query, key, and value vector. The query and key vectors are used to calculate the attention scores, while the value vectors are the representations that will be passed forward.

b) **Attention Scores**: The attention score is calculated by taking the dot product between the query and key vectors and dividing by the square root of the dimension of the key vector. This score determines how much focus should be given to each word in the sequence.

c) **Softmax**: The attention scores are passed through a softmax function to normalize them, ensuring they sum to 1. This allows the model to focus more on the most relevant words while generating the output.

d) **Weighted Sum of Values**: The final output for each word is a weighted sum of the value vectors, where the weights are determined by the attention scores.

The formula for the attention mechanism is:

$$\text{Attention}(Q, K, V) = \text{softmax}\left(\frac{QK^T}{\sqrt{d_k}}\right)V$$

Where:

- Q is the query matrix,
- K is the key matrix,
- V is the value matrix,
- *dk* is the dimension of the key vectors.

Multi-Head Attention

To capture different relationships between words in parallel, transformers use **multi-head attention**, which splits the queries, keys, and values into multiple heads (subspaces) and computes the attention scores independently for each head. The outputs of each head are then concatenated and projected back into the original space.

Graphical Representation of Attention Mechanism:

```
Query --------|     |------- Attention Score ----> Output
                            |      |
                   Key ---------|      |
                            |      |
                   Value ------>|      |
                                   |
                     +----------------------+
                     | Weighted Sum of Values |
                     +----------------------+
```

In the diagram:

- The **query**, **key**, and **value** vectors are derived from the input sequence.
- The attention mechanism computes the weighted sum of values based on the attention score, which is determined by the similarity between the query and the key.

3. Transformer Models and Their Applications

Transformers have become the backbone of state-of-the-art NLP models. Some of the most notable transformer-based models include **BERT**, **GPT**, and **T5**, which have been used for a wide range of NLP tasks such as text classification, machine translation, question answering, and text generation.

BERT (Bidirectional Encoder Representations from Transformers)

BERT, developed by Google, is a pre-trained transformer model that uses a bidirectional attention mechanism to learn contextualized word embeddings. Unlike previous models like Word2Vec, which use a fixed word embedding for each word, BERT dynamically generates word representations based on the surrounding context in a sentence. This allows BERT to handle tasks like **question answering**, **named entity recognition**, and **sentiment analysis** with remarkable accuracy.

- **Pre-training Objective**: BERT is pre-trained on a large corpus of text using a **masked language model (MLM)** objective, where random words are masked, and the model is trained to predict these missing words.

GPT (Generative Pre-trained Transformer)

GPT, developed by OpenAI, is a transformer model trained for **text generation**. Unlike BERT, which is designed for bidirectional context, GPT uses a unidirectional (left-to-right) attention mechanism, making it particularly suitable for generating coherent text. GPT-3, the latest version, has 175 billion parameters and is capable of performing a wide range of tasks with minimal fine-tuning, including **summarization**, **translation**, and **question answering**.

- **Pre-training Objective**: GPT is pre-trained using a **causal language modeling (CLM)** objective, where the model learns to predict the next word in a sequence given the previous words.

T5 (Text-to-Text Transfer Transformer)

T5 is a transformer model developed by Google that treats every NLP task as a **text-to-text** problem. In T5, both the input and output of any task are always text, whether it is a classification task, a translation task, or a question-answering task. This unified approach allows T5 to handle a wide variety of tasks with the same architecture.

4. Advantages of Transformers

a) **Parallelization**: Unlike RNNs, which process one time step at a time, transformers process the entire sequence in parallel, allowing for faster training and more efficient use of computational resources.

b) **Long-Range Dependencies**: The self-attention mechanism enables transformers to capture long-range dependencies between words in a sequence, which is crucial for understanding context in NLP tasks.

c) **Scalability**: Transformers scale well with increasing data and model size. They have been shown to outperform previous models like RNNs and LSTMs on large datasets, especially for tasks that involve complex dependencies.

d) **Transfer Learning**: Transformer models, especially those pre-trained on large corpora (like BERT or GPT), can be fine-tuned on specific tasks with relatively smaller datasets, achieving state-of-the-art performance even with limited task-specific data.

5. Limitations of Transformers

a) **Computational Cost**: The self-attention mechanism requires quadratic time complexity in relation to the sequence length, making transformers computationally expensive for long sequences.

b) **Data Hunger**: Transformer-based models, particularly large ones like GPT-3, require vast amounts of training data, which can be a limitation in some domains where data is scarce.

c) **Interpretability**: While transformers have shown remarkable performance across a wide range of tasks, their decision-making process is still largely opaque, and understanding why a transformer model makes a particular decision remains a challenge.

Conclusion

Transformers and attention mechanisms have fundamentally transformed the landscape of NLP, enabling models to efficiently capture contextual relationships within text and handle long-range dependencies. The success of transformer-based models like BERT, GPT, and T5 has set new benchmarks in a wide variety of NLP tasks, from text generation and translation to question answering and sentiment analysis.

Despite their tremendous success, transformers come with challenges, including high computational costs and the need for large-scale datasets. However, their ability to scale and their superior performance on NLP tasks make them the dominant architecture in modern NLP systems. As research continues to advance, transformers are expected to evolve and further shape the future of natural language understanding.

Chapter 5: Introduction to Transformer Models

Concept and Development

Introduction to Transformer Models

The transformer model, introduced by Vaswani et al. in 2017 in the paper *"Attention is All You Need"*, has fundamentally revolutionized Natural Language Processing (NLP) and deep learning in general. Prior to the transformer's introduction, the dominant approaches to sequence modeling, such as **Recurrent Neural Networks (RNNs)** and **Long Short-Term Memory Networks (LSTMs)**, struggled with issues like vanishing gradients and the inability to handle long-range dependencies effectively. The transformer model, by completely removing the reliance on recurrence and introducing a novel **attention mechanism**, has drastically improved performance across a wide range of NLP tasks.

Transformers have become the backbone of some of the most advanced and widely used NLP models in the world today, such as **BERT**, **GPT**, **T5**, and **RoBERTa**. These models have set new benchmarks in tasks such as machine translation, question answering, sentiment analysis, and text generation, among others.

1. The Motivation Behind Transformer Models

Before transformers, sequential models like **RNNs** and **LSTMs** were widely used for NLP tasks due to their ability to process sequences step by step. These models processed data in a sequential manner, making it difficult to parallelize operations efficiently. Additionally, RNNs and LSTMs struggled to capture long-range dependencies in sequences because of the **vanishing gradient problem**, which limited their performance on tasks involving long documents or complex relationships between words.

Challenges with RNNs and LSTMs:

- **Sequential Processing**: RNNs and LSTMs process input sequences one step at a time, which makes it difficult to parallelize training over sequences. This leads to longer training times and inefficiencies when working with large datasets.
- **Difficulty with Long-Term Dependencies**: While LSTMs were designed to mitigate the vanishing gradient problem, they still struggled to retain information over very long sequences. This made them less effective for tasks like machine translation or document summarization, where context from distant parts of the sequence is important.

In response to these challenges, the transformer model was designed to process sequences in **parallel** and leverage a mechanism that could effectively capture long-range dependencies across the entire sequence. The key innovation behind the transformer is its **self-attention mechanism**, which allows the model to attend to all parts of the sequence simultaneously, regardless of the position of the words.

2. The Transformer Architecture

The transformer architecture is built upon the **self-attention mechanism** and is designed to process entire sequences in parallel. Unlike traditional sequence models, transformers have two main components: the **encoder** and the **decoder**, each consisting of multiple layers of self-attention and feed-forward neural networks.

Key Components of the Transformer Model:

1. **Self-Attention**: The self-attention mechanism allows the model to weigh the importance of different words in the input sequence relative to each other. Each word in the sequence can attend to all other words, enabling the model to capture relationships and dependencies, regardless of their position in the sequence.

  - The attention mechanism computes an attention score for each word in the sequence, which indicates how much focus should be placed on each word when generating the output. This allows the model to make decisions based on the full context of the sentence, rather than just relying on adjacent words.

2. **Multi-Head Attention**: Rather than using a single attention mechanism, transformers use **multi-head attention**, which runs multiple attention mechanisms in parallel. Each attention head can focus on different parts of the sequence, allowing the model to capture different types of relationships between words.

3. **Positional Encoding**: Since transformers process the entire sequence in parallel, they do not have an inherent understanding of the word order in the sequence (unlike RNNs or LSTMs). To address this, positional encodings are added to the input embeddings to provide information about the relative position of each word in the sequence.

4. **Feed-Forward Neural Networks**: After the attention mechanism, the transformer includes a position-wise **feed-forward neural network** that processes the output of the attention mechanism. This consists of two linear layers with a ReLU activation in between.

5. **Layer Normalization and Residual Connections**: To stabilize training, the transformer model includes **residual connections** and **layer normalization** at each sub-layer (self-attention and feed-forward networks). This helps to prevent vanishing gradients and ensures more efficient training.

The Transformer Encoder-Decoder Architecture:

1. **Encoder**:
   - The encoder takes an input sequence (such as a sentence) and processes it through multiple layers of self-attention and feed-forward neural networks.
   - The encoder generates a set of **hidden representations** that capture contextual information about each word in the sequence.
2. **Decoder**:
   - The decoder uses the output of the encoder along with its own previously generated outputs to produce the final sequence (such as a translated sentence).
   - The decoder performs **masked self-attention** (i.e., attending to earlier words in the sequence) and uses the encoder's hidden representations via **encoder-decoder attention** to generate the final output.

3. The Self-Attention Mechanism

The attention mechanism allows the transformer to focus on different parts of the sequence when producing an output. Here's how the self-attention mechanism works:

1. **Input Representations**: Each word in the input sequence is represented as an embedding, and the model learns three vectors for each word: **Query (Q)**, **Key (K)**, and **Value (V)**. These vectors are computed by applying learned weight matrices to the input embeddings.
2. **Attention Score Calculation**: The attention score for each pair of words in the sequence is computed as the dot product of the query vector of one word and the key vector of another word:

$$\text{Attention Score}(Q, K) = \frac{QK^T}{\sqrt{d_k}}$$

where dk is the dimension of the key vector, and the resulting score determines the relevance of the two words.

3. **Softmax**: The attention scores are passed through a **softmax function** to normalize them, ensuring that the weights sum to 1. This provides a probability distribution that determines how much focus should be placed on each word in the sequence.
4. **Weighted Sum**: The final output for each word is the weighted sum of the value vectors, where the weights are determined by the attention scores.

Graphical Representation of Self-Attention:

```
Query      |     |     Attention Score  ---> Weighted Sum

                |     |

Key   --->|     |

                |     |

Value --->|     |
```

The **query**, **key**, and **value** vectors are generated from the input embeddings, and the attention mechanism computes the attention score to determine the importance of each word in relation to others.

4. Development of Transformer Models

The introduction of the transformer model has led to the development of many groundbreaking models in NLP. Some of the most important transformer-based models include:

BERT (Bidirectional Encoder Representations from Transformers)

- **BERT** is a transformer-based model that was pre-trained on large text corpora using a **masked language model (MLM)** objective. This means that during training, certain words in the sentence are randomly masked, and the model is tasked with predicting the missing words based on the context provided by both the left and right sides of the sentence.
- **Bidirectional Attention**: Unlike previous models (e.g., GPT), which process text in a unidirectional (left-to-right) manner, BERT uses bidirectional attention, making it better suited for understanding the context of words in a sentence.
- **Applications**: BERT has been fine-tuned for various NLP tasks, including **question answering**, **sentiment analysis**, and **named entity recognition**.

GPT (Generative Pre-trained Transformer)

- **GPT** is a unidirectional (left-to-right) transformer model trained using a **causal language modeling (CLM)** objective. GPT is pre-trained to predict the next word in a sequence given the previous words.
- **Unidirectional Attention**: GPT processes the input text in a left-to-right manner, meaning that the model generates the output word by word, predicting the next word in the sequence.
- **Applications**: GPT has been widely used for **text generation**, **summarization**, and **dialog systems**.

T5 (Text-to-Text Transfer Transformer)

- **T5** takes a novel approach by treating all NLP tasks as a **text-to-text** problem, where both the input and output are always text. For example, for a translation task, the input might be "translate

English to French: How are you?", and the output would be the translated sentence.

- **Unified Framework**: By using the text-to-text framework, T5 can be fine-tuned for a wide variety of NLP tasks without task-specific architectures.

5. Advantages of Transformer Models

a) **Parallelization**: Unlike RNNs and LSTMs, transformers process the entire sequence in parallel, which allows for faster training and more efficient use of computational resources.

b) **Long-Range Dependencies**: The self-attention mechanism enables transformers to capture dependencies between words at different positions in the sequence, regardless of how far apart they are. This is particularly useful in NLP tasks that require understanding context over long passages.

c) **Scalability**: Transformers scale well with increasing model size and dataset size. They have shown consistent improvements with larger models and more data, making them highly effective for large-scale NLP tasks.

d) **Flexibility**: Transformer models can be adapted for a wide variety of tasks, including classification, generation, and translation, without the need for task-specific architectures.

Transformer models have fundamentally changed the landscape of NLP by introducing the self-attention mechanism, which allows for parallel processing and the efficient handling of long-range dependencies. The development of transformer-based models like BERT, GPT, and T5 has set new performance benchmarks in NLP, achieving state-of-the-art results in a variety of tasks.

While transformers have revolutionized NLP, they come with challenges, such as high computational costs and the need for large datasets. However, the benefits they provide in terms of scalability, flexibility, and performance make them the architecture of choice for many modern NLP systems. As research in transformers continues to evolve, these models will likely remain at the forefront of natural language understanding and generation.

Architecture - Encoders, Decoders, Attention Layers

Introduction

The **transformer model** has redefined how we approach sequence modeling in Natural Language Processing (NLP) by introducing a new architecture that does not rely on recurrence, unlike Recurrent Neural Networks (RNNs) and Long Short-Term Memory networks (LSTMs). Instead, transformers rely entirely on a mechanism called **self-attention**, which allows for capturing relationships between words in a sequence more efficiently. The transformer architecture, as introduced by Vaswani et al. in the 2017 paper *"Attention is All You Need"*, is the foundation of many state-of-the-art models, such as **BERT**, **GPT**, **T5**, and others.

At the core of the transformer architecture are two main components:

1. **Encoder**
2. **Decoder**

These components, in turn, are built from the **attention layers**, which are the main mechanism through which the transformer processes and learns relationships in sequential data.

1. Overview of Transformer Architecture

The transformer model is based on the idea of **self-attention**, which allows it to weigh the importance of different words in the input sequence and capture dependencies between words regardless of their position. Unlike RNNs or LSTMs, transformers process the entire sequence in parallel, making them more computationally efficient.

The architecture of the transformer model consists of two main parts:

1. **Encoder**: Processes the input sequence and encodes it into a set of context-aware representations.
2. **Decoder**: Takes the encoded representations and generates the output sequence (such as in machine translation, where the input is a sentence in one language, and the output is the translation in another language).

The transformer uses multiple layers of encoders and decoders, with each layer containing self-attention and feed-forward neural network sub-layers.

Transformer Encoder-Decoder Structure:

- **Encoder**: The encoder processes the input sequence and produces a set of hidden representations (contextualized word embeddings).
- **Decoder**: The decoder takes these hidden representations and uses them to generate the output sequence, one word at a time.

The key innovation in transformers is the self-attention mechanism, which enables both the encoder and decoder to capture relationships between all words in the sequence, regardless of their position.

2. Transformer Encoder: Understanding the Encoder Layer

The **encoder** is responsible for transforming the input sequence into a set of contextually enriched representations that capture relationships between words in the sequence. The encoder consists of multiple layers (typically 6 or more), and each layer is made up of two main sub-layers:

1. **Multi-Head Self-Attention**
2. **Position-wise Feed-Forward Networks**

Components of the Encoder Layer:

1. **Multi-Head Self-Attention**: The self-attention mechanism allows each word in the input sequence to "attend" to all other words, assigning different weights based on the relevance of other words in the sequence. In this mechanism, each word is represented by three vectors: **Query (Q)**, **Key (K)**, and **Value (V)**. Self-attention computes the attention score between each pair of words, determining how much focus each word should give to other words in the sequence.
   - **Multi-Head Attention**: Rather than using a single attention mechanism, the transformer employs **multi-head attention,** where multiple attention mechanisms are run in parallel. Each attention head focuses on different aspects of the input sequence, allowing the model to capture diverse relationships between words. The outputs of all attention heads are concatenated and linearly transformed.
2. **Position-wise Feed-Forward Network**: After the attention mechanism, the transformer applies a feed-forward neural network to each position (word) in the sequence. This consists of two fully connected layers, with a **ReLU activation** in between.
3. **Residual Connection and Layer Normalization**: Each sub-layer (self-attention and feed-forward network) has a **residual connection** around it, followed by **layer normalization**. The residual connection helps avoid the vanishing gradient problem, and the layer normalization stabilizes the learning process.

The Encoder Layer in Detail:

- **Input**: The input sequence (a sequence of word embeddings or token representations) is passed through the encoder.
- **Self-Attention**: Each word in the sequence computes attention scores with respect to every other word and adjusts its representation accordingly.
- **Feed-Forward Network**: The updated representations from the attention mechanism are passed through the feed-forward network.
- **Output**: The output is a sequence of context-aware embeddings that represent each word in relation to all others in the sequence.

Graphical Representation of the Encoder:

```
Input Sequence  ---> [Multi-Head Self-Attention] ---> [Feed-Forward Network] ---> Output Sequence
          |                      |                          |
          +----------------------+--------------------------+
                         |                |
               Residual + Layer Norm  + Residual + Layer Norm
```

In the diagram, the encoder processes the input sequence through multiple layers of self-attention and feed-forward networks, with residual connections and layer normalization applied at each stage.

3. Transformer Decoder: Understanding the Decoder Layer

The **decoder** in the transformer model generates the output sequence from the encoded representations produced by the encoder. Like the encoder, the decoder consists of multiple layers (typically 6 or more), and each layer contains three sub-layers:

a) **Masked Multi-Head Self-Attention**

b) **Multi-Head Attention (Encoder-Decoder Attention)**

c) **Position-wise Feed-Forward Networks**

Components of the Decoder Layer:

A. **Masked Multi-Head Self-Attention**: In the decoder, the self-attention mechanism is **masked** to ensure that the model does not look ahead at future words when generating a word in the sequence. The masked attention prevents the model from cheating during training by having access to future tokens.

   - Like the encoder, the decoder uses **multi-head attention** to process multiple aspects of the sequence simultaneously. The difference is that the decoder attends to both previous words in the sequence and the encoded representations from the encoder.

B. **Encoder-Decoder Attention**: In this layer, the decoder attends to the encoder's output. This enables the decoder to focus on relevant parts of the input sequence when generating the output sequence. The attention mechanism here is similar to the self-attention used in the encoder but uses the encoder's hidden states as the keys and values.

C. **Feed-Forward Network**: Similar to the encoder, the decoder also includes a position-wise feed-forward network, which processes the output of the attention layers.

D. **Residual Connections and Layer Normalization**: Like in the encoder, the decoder layers use residual connections and layer normalization to stabilize the training process and prevent the vanishing gradient problem.

The Decoder Layer in Detail:

- **Input**: The decoder receives the previous output (during inference, this could be the generated word) and the encoded representations from the encoder.

- **Masked Self-Attention**: The decoder computes attention scores with respect to previous words in the output sequence, ensuring it doesn't cheat by looking ahead.
- **Encoder-Decoder Attention**: The decoder also computes attention scores with respect to the encoder's hidden states to generate contextually appropriate output words.
- **Feed-Forward Network**: The updated representations are passed through a feed-forward network.
- **Output**: The final output is the generated sequence of words.

Graphical Representation of the Decoder:

```
Input Sequence (from Encoder) ---> [Masked Multi-Head Self-Attention] --->
[Encoder-Decoder Attention] ---> [Feed-Forward Network] ---> Output Sequence

        |                   |                    |                    |
        +-------------------------+-------------------------+---------------------------+
                      |             |
          Residual + Layer Norm  + Residual + Layer Norm
```

In the diagram, the decoder works similarly to the encoder but with the additional encoder-decoder attention, allowing the decoder to attend to the encoder's output while generating the final sequence.

4. Attention Mechanism: The Heart of Transformers

The **attention mechanism** is the key innovation of the transformer model. It allows the model to focus on different parts of the input sequence, attending to relevant words when generating output. In the case of self-attention, every word in the sequence is assigned a weight that indicates how much attention it should pay to each of the other words.

Self-Attention Process:

1. **Query, Key, Value Vectors**: For each word in the sequence, we compute three vectors: **Query (Q)**, **Key (K)**, and **Value (V)**. These vectors are used to compute attention scores.
2. **Attention Score Calculation**: The attention score is calculated as the dot product between the query and key vectors, followed by a softmax operation to normalize the scores.
3. **Weighted Sum**: The final output for each word is the weighted sum of the value vectors, where the weights are determined by the attention scores.

Multi-Head Attention:

To capture different relationships in the sequence, transformers use **multi-head attention**, where multiple attention mechanisms operate in parallel. Each head focuses on different parts of the sequence, capturing different dependencies.

Graphical Representation of Attention:

```
     Input Sequence

          |

   +---------------+

   |   Query (Q)   |

   +---------------+

          |

   +---------------+

   |    Key (K)    |

   +---------------+
```

```
        |
+----------------+
|   Value (V)    |
+----------------+
        |
  Attention Scores
        |
  Weighted Sum of Values
```

In the diagram:

- Each word in the sequence is represented by a query, key, and value.
- Attention scores are computed by comparing the query with the key, and the result is used to weigh the values.

5. Advantages of Transformer Architecture

a) **Parallelization**: Unlike RNNs and LSTMs, which process data sequentially, transformers process the entire sequence in parallel, enabling much faster training and inference.

b) **Long-Range Dependencies**: The self-attention mechanism enables transformers to capture long-range dependencies across the entire sequence, making them more effective for tasks that require global context.

c) **Scalability**: Transformers scale efficiently with increasing data and model size, outperforming older architectures like RNNs and LSTMs as the size of the dataset grows.

d) **Flexibility**: Transformers can be adapted to a variety of NLP tasks by fine-tuning pre-trained models such as BERT and GPT, making them highly versatile.

The introduction of transformer models has revolutionized NLP by replacing the sequential nature of RNNs and LSTMs with a more efficient and scalable architecture based on self-attention mechanisms. By enabling parallel processing and effectively capturing long-range dependencies, transformers have set new benchmarks in NLP tasks such as machine translation, text generation, and question answering.

The key components of the transformer architecture - the encoder, decoder, and attention layers - work together to provide a powerful framework for understanding and generating language. As transformer-based models continue to evolve, they will remain at the forefront of advancements in natural language understanding, powering many of the most advanced AI systems today.

Transformer Variants

Since the introduction of the **transformer model** in the seminal paper *"Attention is All You Need"* by Vaswani et al. in 2017, the architecture has rapidly evolved and diversified. The core concept of the transformer — based on **self-attention** — has led to a range of **transformer variants** that address specific challenges or improve on the original model's architecture. These variants have become foundational in achieving state-of-the-art performance across a wide variety of Natural Language Processing (NLP) tasks, such as machine translation, text generation, summarization, and more.

1. BERT (Bidirectional Encoder Representations from Transformers)

Overview

BERT, introduced by Google in 2018, is one of the most influential transformer variants. While the original transformer model uses both an encoder and a decoder, BERT uses only the **encoder** portion of the transformer architecture. The key innovation in BERT lies in its **bidirectional attention mechanism**, which enables the model to capture contextual relationships in both directions - from left to right and from right to left - when processing sequences.

Key Features of BERT:

a) **Bidirectional Attention**: Unlike earlier models like GPT, which used unidirectional attention (left-to-right), BERT uses bidirectional attention, meaning it considers both the left and right context for each word in a sequence. This bidirectional context allows BERT to better understand the meaning of each word, especially when words have multiple meanings depending on context.

b) **Masked Language Modeling (MLM)**: During training, BERT randomly masks out words in a sentence and learns to predict the masked words based on the surrounding context. This allows BERT to learn deep contextual relationships between words.

c) **Pre-training and Fine-tuning**: BERT is pre-trained on large corpora of text using MLM and a next-sentence prediction task, and then fine-tuned on specific downstream tasks (e.g., sentiment analysis, question answering, etc.). This transfer learning approach allows BERT to perform well on a wide range of NLP tasks with relatively small task-specific datasets.

Graphical Representation of BERT:

Input Sequence --> [Bidirectional Attention (Self-Attention)] --> [Feed-Forward Network] --> Output Sequence

|

[Masking & Next-Sentence Prediction]

In this diagram, the bidirectional attention mechanism allows BERT to learn from both the left and right context of a word, and it is pre-trained with a focus on masked language modeling.

2. GPT (Generative Pre-trained Transformer)

Overview

GPT, developed by OpenAI, is a unidirectional transformer variant designed specifically for text generation tasks. GPT uses the **decoder** portion of the original transformer architecture and applies **causal language modeling** (predicting the next word based on previous words) during pre-training. This unidirectional approach makes GPT particularly suited for text generation tasks where the model must predict one word at a time in a sequence.

Key Features of GPT:

a) **Unidirectional Attention**: GPT uses **left-to-right attention**, meaning it only considers the previous context (to the left of the current word) when predicting the next word. This is ideal for text generation tasks, where the goal is to generate coherent and contextually relevant text.

b) **Autoregressive Pre-training**: GPT is trained using an autoregressive language model objective, where it learns to predict the next word in a sequence given the words before it. During pre-training, GPT is fed large amounts of text and learns to model the distribution of word sequences.

c) **Fine-tuning for Specific Tasks**: After pre-training, GPT can be fine-tuned on specific NLP tasks, such as summarization, translation, or question answering. The model is highly flexible and can be adapted to a variety of text-based applications.

Graphical Representation of GPT:

```
Input Sequence --> [Causal Self-Attention (Unidirectional)] --> [Feed-Forward Network] --> Output Sequence

        |

   [Predict Next Word]
```

In this diagram, GPT uses unidirectional self-attention to generate text, considering only the previous words when predicting the next word.

3. T5 (Text-to-Text Transfer Transformer)

Overview

T5, developed by Google, is a transformer model designed to handle **all NLP tasks as a text-to-text problem**. Unlike BERT and GPT, which are designed for specific tasks like masked language modeling or autoregressive text generation, T5 treats both the input and output of every task as text. For example, for a translation task, the input might be "Translate English to French: How are you?" and the output would be the translated sentence in French.

Key Features of T5:

a) **Unified Text-to-Text Framework**: T5's novel approach is to convert all NLP tasks into text generation problems. Whether it's question answering, text classification, or summarization, the input and output are always text. This allows T5 to handle a wide range of tasks without needing task-specific architectures.

b) **Pre-training on Multiple Tasks**: T5 is pre-trained on a massive dataset, using a denoising autoencoder objective, where parts of the input text are masked, and the model learns to predict the missing parts. This pre-training is task-agnostic, meaning it helps the model generalize across a wide variety of tasks.

c) **Fine-Tuning**: After pre-training, T5 can be fine-tuned for specific tasks by simply changing the task prompt. For example, for summarization, the prompt could be "summarize: [text]," and for translation, the prompt could be "translate: [text]."

Graphical Representation of T5:

Input Text --> [Text-to-Text Processing] --> [Transformer Model] --> Output Text

|

[Task-Specific Prompt]

In the diagram, T5 uses a unified text-to-text framework, where each task is converted into a text generation problem. This allows for a flexible model that can be adapted to a wide range of NLP tasks.

4. RoBERTa (Robustly Optimized BERT Pre-training Approach)

Overview

RoBERTa, developed by Facebook AI, is a variant of BERT that aims to improve upon BERT's pre-training procedure by exploring several hyperparameter changes and training on a much larger dataset. RoBERTa removes the next-sentence prediction task used in BERT and trains on larger batches, more data, and for longer periods of time.

Key Features of RoBERTa:

a) **No Next-Sentence Prediction**: RoBERTa eliminates BERT's next-sentence prediction task, which was found to have little effect on model performance. Instead, it focuses entirely on masked language modeling.

b) **Larger Datasets and Longer Training**: RoBERTa was trained on a larger dataset (160GB of text) and for longer periods of time, which allows it to learn richer representations of language.

c) **Dynamic Masking**: Unlike BERT, where the masking was fixed during training, RoBERTa uses dynamic masking, meaning that each training instance could have different words masked out, which increases the model's ability to generalize.

Graphical Representation of RoBERTa:

Input Sequence --> [Bidirectional Self-Attention] --> [Feed-Forward Network] --> Output Sequence

|

[Masked Language Modeling]

In this diagram, RoBERTa uses a modified version of BERT's architecture, with improvements in the pre-training phase, including dynamic masking and longer training.

5. DistilBERT

Overview

DistilBERT is a smaller and faster version of BERT, developed through a technique called **knowledge distillation**. The goal of DistilBERT is to retain most of BERT's performance while significantly reducing the model's size and computational requirements. This makes it a good choice for deploying BERT-like models in resource-constrained environments.

Key Features of DistilBERT:

a) **Knowledge Distillation**: DistilBERT is trained using a teacher-student paradigm, where a smaller "student" model (DistilBERT) is trained to mimic the behavior of a larger "teacher" model (BERT). This results in a model that is both smaller and faster but still performs comparably to BERT.

b) **Smaller and Faster**: DistilBERT reduces the size of BERT by 60% and speeds up inference while retaining 97% of BERT's language understanding capabilities.

Graphical Representation of DistilBERT:

Input Sequence --> [Bidirectional Self-Attention (Distilled)] --> [Feed-Forward Network] --> Output Sequence

|

[Knowledge Distillation]

In the diagram, DistilBERT performs the same tasks as BERT but with a smaller architecture, making it more suitable for deployment in production environments.

Conclusion

Transformer models have become the cornerstone of modern NLP, providing powerful, flexible, and efficient ways to process sequential data. Since the introduction of the original transformer model, many variants have been developed to address specific challenges or improve performance. Each of these transformer variants - **BERT**, **GPT**, **T5**, **RoBERTa**, and **DistilBERT** - offers unique innovations that have contributed to pushing the boundaries of NLP and machine learning.

The development of these models highlights the growing importance of transformers in the field, with applications ranging from language understanding and generation to question answering and translation. As transformer models continue to evolve, we can expect further advancements that will enhance their performance and enable more sophisticated language tasks.

Chapter 6: Pre-Training Large Language Models

Purpose and Significance of Pre-Training

The process of pre-training **large language models (LLMs)** has become a critical step in the development of modern Natural Language Processing (NLP) systems. Pre-training allows models to learn rich language representations from massive amounts of unstructured text data, which they can then fine-tune for specific downstream tasks such as sentiment analysis, machine translation, or text summarization. In recent years, models like **BERT**, **GPT**, and **T5** have demonstrated that pre-training on large corpora can lead to dramatic improvements in performance across a wide range of tasks.

Pre-training has become the foundation for achieving state-of-the-art results in NLP. The ability to pre-train a model on general language data and later fine-tune it for specialized tasks is a major factor in the success of transformer-based models.

1. Purpose of Pre-Training Large Language Models

Pre-training is the first phase of training a large language model and is typically performed using a **self-supervised learning** approach. The main goal of pre-training is to expose the model to vast amounts of textual data in an unsupervised manner, allowing it to learn general language patterns and structures before being fine-tuned on specific tasks.

Key Objectives of Pre-Training:

a) **Learning General Language Representations**:
Pre-training helps a model learn general language representations that capture the nuances of syntax, grammar, semantics, and context. This involves learning the relationships between words, phrases, and sentences, and how different parts of text relate to one another.

b) **Developing Contextual Understanding**:
Language is inherently contextual. Words can have different meanings depending on the context in which they appear. Through pre-training, a model learns to encode context-dependent meanings of words and phrases, which is essential for understanding text at a deeper level.

c) **Improving Transfer Learning**:
One of the major advantages of pre-training is that it enables **transfer learning**. Once a model is pre-trained on a large corpus of text, it can be fine-tuned on smaller, task-specific datasets to improve performance. This makes it possible to train high-performing models even in domains where annotated data is scarce.

d) **Reducing the Need for Labeled Data**:
Pre-training enables the model to learn from unannotated data, which is abundant and easily accessible, as opposed to relying on labor-intensive labeled datasets. After pre-training, the model can be fine-tuned on labeled data for specific tasks, which is often a much smaller dataset compared to what would be needed for training a model from scratch.

2. Significance of Pre-Training for Large Language Models

The significance of pre-training in the development of LLMs is multifaceted. Pre-training allows the model to generalize better, achieve higher accuracy, and become more adaptable to a variety of NLP tasks. This process is the foundation for models like **BERT** and **GPT**, which are capable of transferring their learning from a general corpus to specific tasks with minimal task-specific adjustments.

Key Reasons Pre-Training is Significant:

a) **Learning from Vast Amounts of Data**:
Pre-training enables large language models to learn from vast amounts of diverse text data (often billions or trillions of words).

By exposing the model to this large corpus, it becomes capable of understanding a wide range of linguistic phenomena, including idiomatic expressions, synonyms, syntactic structures, and long-range dependencies.

- **Example**: In pre-training, a model might learn that "bank" can refer to a financial institution or the side of a river depending on the context, which is critical for tasks like **word sense disambiguation**.

b) **Improved Generalization Across Tasks**:
Pre-trained models can generalize well across different tasks because they have already learned a broad understanding of language. After pre-training, the model can be fine-tuned for a specific task (e.g., sentiment analysis or text classification) with fewer task-specific examples, thanks to its strong foundation in language understanding.

c) **Enabling Multi-Task Learning**:
Pre-training also facilitates multi-task learning, where a model can be fine-tuned on several tasks simultaneously. Since the model has already learned rich, general language representations during pre-training, it can easily adapt to multiple tasks without needing separate models for each one.

d) **Faster Convergence in Fine-Tuning**:
Pre-trained models converge faster when fine-tuned on a specific task compared to training from scratch. This is because the model has already learned important language features during pre-training, and fine-tuning only requires adjusting the model to the nuances of the task at hand.

e) **Creating a Solid Language Foundation**:
Pre-training on large text corpora allows the model to build a foundational understanding of how words and sentences are structured. This understanding serves as the basis for more

complex NLP tasks, such as language translation, question answering, and text generation.

3. How Pre-Training Works: A Closer Look at Self-Supervised Learning

Pre-training in the context of LLMs typically relies on **self-supervised learning**, a form of unsupervised learning where the model learns from the data itself without needing manually labeled examples. In self-supervised learning, the model generates pseudo-labels from the input data, allowing it to learn useful representations for downstream tasks.

Common Pre-Training Objectives:

a) **Masked Language Modeling (MLM)** (used in BERT):

- In **MLM**, a certain percentage of the words in the input sequence are randomly replaced with a special **[MASK]** token. The model is then tasked with predicting the original words based on the surrounding context. This approach allows the model to learn bidirectional contextual relationships.
- **Example**: Given the sentence "The cat sat on the [MASK]", the model must predict the word "mat".

b) **Causal Language Modeling (Autoregressive Modeling)** (used in GPT):

- In **causal language modeling**, the model is trained to predict the next word in a sequence given the previous words. The model is trained autoregressively, meaning it generates text one word at a time, using the previous words as context.
- **Example**: Given the sentence "The cat sat on the", the model predicts the next word, such as "mat".

c) **Denoising Autoencoding** (used in T5):

- In **denoising autoencoding**, a portion of the input sequence is randomly masked or corrupted, and the model is trained to reconstruct the original, clean input from the noisy version. This approach is similar to BERT's MLM but can be applied to more complex tasks.
- **Example**: In a text-to-text framework, the input might be "Translate English to French: How are you?" with parts of the sentence removed, and the model must reconstruct the full sentence.

4. The Process of Pre-Training Large Language Models

Pre-training large language models involves training them on vast amounts of text data, which allows them to learn language representations. Below is a typical pre-training pipeline:

a) **Data Collection**: A large and diverse corpus of text data is gathered. This data can come from books, articles, websites, and other unstructured text sources. Common datasets for pre-training include **Wikipedia**, **BooksCorpus**, **Common Crawl**, and **OpenWebText**.

b) **Tokenization and Embedding**: The text is tokenized into subword units or words. Each token is then mapped to a high-dimensional vector (embedding), which represents its meaning in the model's learned space.

c) **Masking or Corruption (for MLM and Denoising Tasks)**: Some tokens are masked or corrupted in the input data. For instance, in BERT's masked language modeling task, random tokens are replaced with the **[MASK]** token.

d) **Model Training**: The model is trained to predict the masked or missing tokens using a specific pre-training objective, such as masked language modeling or causal language modeling. The model adjusts its weights to minimize the prediction error.

e) **Fine-Tuning (Optional)**: Once the model is pre-trained, it can be fine-tuned on a smaller, task-specific dataset to adapt to specific tasks, such as sentiment analysis, machine translation, or named entity recognition. Fine-tuning involves training the model on labeled data for specific NLP tasks, often requiring much fewer examples due to the pre-trained language representations.

5. Benefits of Pre-Training

a) **Generalization to Unseen Tasks**: Pre-trained models generalize well to tasks that they were not specifically trained on. This is because they have learned a wide range of linguistic patterns during pre-training that can be transferred to a variety of downstream tasks.

b) **Reduced Data Requirements**: Pre-training reduces the amount of task-specific labeled data required for fine-tuning. Since the model already has general knowledge of language, fine-tuning can be done with fewer labeled examples.

c) **Efficiency in Training**: Pre-training on a large corpus and fine-tuning on smaller task-specific datasets is much more efficient than training from scratch for each task. This reduces both the time and computational resources required.

d) **Transfer Learning**: Pre-trained models can be fine-tuned to perform multiple tasks, making them highly versatile. Transfer learning allows models to be easily adapted for applications like **question answering, text summarization**, and **speech-to-text** with minimal additional training.

6. Challenges in Pre-Training Large Language Models

a) **Computational Cost**: Pre-training large language models requires significant computational resources, including powerful

GPUs and TPUs, as well as large-scale storage and memory. This makes pre-training expensive and often accessible only to large organizations.

b) **Environmental Impact**: Training large language models on massive datasets requires enormous energy consumption, contributing to the environmental footprint of AI research. This is an increasing concern, leading to efforts to make pre-training more efficient.

c) **Bias in Data**: The model learns from large corpora of text, which can include biased or problematic content. Pre-trained models can inherit and even amplify these biases, leading to ethical challenges when deploying these models in real-world applications.

d) **Data Privacy**: Large-scale pre-training typically uses publicly available text, which might inadvertently include sensitive information. This raises concerns about privacy and the use of private data in training large models.

Pre-training is a crucial step in the development of large language models. It allows these models to learn general language representations from vast amounts of unstructured text data, making them highly adaptable and capable of performing well on a variety of NLP tasks. Through pre-training, models like BERT, GPT, and T5 can transfer learned knowledge to specific tasks, reducing the need for large amounts of labeled data and accelerating the development of high-performing NLP systems.

While pre-training has significantly advanced the state-of-the-art in NLP, challenges such as high computational costs, environmental impact, and biases in data remain. Nonetheless, pre-training has proven to be one of the most effective strategies for building powerful language models, and ongoing research is likely to improve both the efficiency and accessibility of this approach in the future.

Methods and Strategies for Pre-Training

Pre-training large language models (LLMs) is a critical phase in developing modern NLP systems. The goal of pre-training is to expose the model to vast amounts of unstructured data, allowing it to learn general linguistic representations that can be fine-tuned for specific downstream tasks. However, pre-training LLMs involves several methods and strategies that differ in their objectives, architecture, and training approaches. These methods have evolved as the need for more efficient, scalable, and task-adaptive models has grown.

1. Pre-Training Objectives: The Core of Pre-Training Methods

The central idea of pre-training is to use a **self-supervised** learning approach where the model learns from large-scale unannotated text data without requiring manual labels. The key component of this is the **pre-training objective**, which defines what the model learns during the pre-training phase.

a) Masked Language Modeling (MLM)

Masked Language Modeling is a pre-training objective used primarily in **BERT**-like models. In MLM, random words in a sentence are masked, and the model is tasked with predicting the masked words based on the surrounding context. This process allows the model to learn bidirectional context, as it uses both the left and right context around the masked word to make predictions.

How MLM Works:

1. The input text is tokenized, and a percentage of tokens are randomly selected and replaced with a **[MASK]** token.
2. The model predicts the original token (word) at the masked position.

3. The loss function is computed based on the model's ability to correctly predict the masked word.

Example:

- Input sentence: "The cat sat on the [MASK]."
- The model needs to predict that the masked word is "mat."

MLM is effective because it forces the model to understand the full context of the sentence, including both preceding and succeeding words. This enables the model to generate richer representations of the input text, useful for a variety of downstream tasks.

b) Causal Language Modeling (CLM)

Causal Language Modeling, used primarily in **GPT** models, is an autoregressive pre-training objective. In CLM, the model learns to predict the next word in a sequence based on the words that came before it, i.e., it processes the sequence **left-to-right**. This type of training is designed to model text generation tasks, where the goal is to predict the next token (word) in a sequence during inference.

How CLM Works:

1. The model is given a sequence of words and predicts the next word at each time step.
2. The training is performed autoregressively, meaning the model uses previously generated words as input to predict the next word in the sequence.

Example:

- Input sentence: "The cat sat on the"
- The model predicts the next word, such as "mat."

CLM is particularly useful for generative tasks, as it allows models to generate new text one word at a time. However, since it is unidirectional (left-to-right), it only learns from past context, unlike bidirectional models like BERT.

c) Denoising Autoencoding

Denoising Autoencoding is a pre-training objective used in models like **T5**. The goal of this method is to introduce noise (e.g., by randomly masking or corrupting parts of the input) and teach the model to recover the original, uncorrupted input. This helps the model learn robust representations of the input, making it adaptable to a wide variety of downstream tasks, such as text generation and machine translation.

How Denoising Autoencoding Works:

1. Random portions of the input sequence are masked or corrupted.
2. The model is trained to reconstruct the original, clean input sequence from the noisy version.
3. The loss function computes the error between the model's output and the original sequence.

Example:

- Input: "Translate English to French: How are you?"
- The model may receive a corrupted version like "Translate English to [MASK]: How are [MASK]?"
- The model is tasked with reconstructing the original text, learning how to recover missing parts.

This strategy is especially useful for text-to-text models, such as **T5**, which are trained to handle a wide range of NLP tasks by treating them all as text generation tasks.

d) Next-Sentence Prediction (NSP)

Next-Sentence Prediction is a task used in **BERT**-like models, where the model learns to predict whether two sentences are consecutive or not. This pre-training objective is designed to capture relationships between sentences in addition to understanding word-level semantics. Although NSP was originally part of BERT's pre-training objective, recent findings suggest that its contribution to performance may not be as significant as initially thought, leading to the development of models like **RoBERTa**, which removed NSP in favor of longer pre-training and more data.

How NSP Works:

1. During training, the model is presented with two sentences, where 50% of the time the second sentence is the true next sentence, and 50% of the time it is randomly selected from other parts of the corpus.
2. The model learns to predict if the second sentence follows the first one.

Example:

- Sentence pair 1: "The cat sat on the mat. It is a cozy spot."
- Sentence pair 2: "The cat sat on the mat. He loves playing outside."
- The model must predict whether the second sentence is likely to follow the first one.

2. Strategies for Pre-Training Large Language Models

While the pre-training objectives are essential for learning effective language representations, the **pre-training strategy** involves additional aspects that influence the performance and efficiency of the model. These strategies include decisions related to dataset construction, training time, batch size, and multi-task learning.

a) Dataset Construction for Pre-Training

The quality and diversity of the dataset used for pre-training is crucial in helping the model learn rich and generalized language representations. Pre-training large language models typically involves large and diverse datasets that cover a wide variety of domains, topics, and linguistic features.

Common Datasets for Pre-Training:

- **Wikipedia**: Provides high-quality, general knowledge text.
- **Common Crawl**: A large-scale web scraping dataset that includes data from a wide variety of sources across the internet.
- **BooksCorpus**: A dataset of books that helps the model learn more complex structures and narratives.
- **OpenWebText**: A dataset derived from web pages, focusing on social media and internet-based content.

The use of diverse, large-scale datasets enables the model to learn a broad understanding of language, which it can then fine-tune for specific tasks.

b) Training on Large Datasets and Longer Training Times

Large-scale models like **GPT-3** and **BERT-large** require extensive computational resources to train. This involves using **massive amounts of text data** and **long training times**. Pre-training on such large datasets ensures that the model can learn rich and robust language representations.

Example: GPT-3 was trained on **570GB** of text data, which required substantial computational power and many weeks of training time. The size and diversity of the data enable GPT-3 to capture a wide range of linguistic features.

c) Fine-Tuning After Pre-Training

While pre-training teaches the model general language representations, **fine-tuning** on task-specific datasets is essential for achieving high performance on downstream tasks. Fine-tuning typically involves adapting the pre-trained model to a specific task, such as sentiment analysis, text classification, or machine translation.

Example:

- **Pre-training**: BERT is pre-trained using Masked Language Modeling (MLM) on a massive corpus.
- **Fine-tuning**: BERT is then fine-tuned on a specific task, such as classifying movie reviews into positive and negative categories using a smaller labeled dataset.

This two-step process allows LLMs to perform well on a wide variety of tasks with relatively little task-specific data.

d) Multi-Task Pre-Training

In **multi-task pre-training**, models are trained to solve multiple tasks simultaneously, allowing them to generalize better to various types of NLP problems. This strategy involves training the model on a mixture of tasks (e.g., language modeling, classification, and translation) rather than focusing on a single task.

Benefits of Multi-Task Pre-Training:

- **Task Generalization**: The model learns representations that are useful for a variety of tasks, improving its ability to generalize across domains.
- **More Efficient Use of Data**: By training on multiple tasks at once, the model can learn more efficiently, using the same data for different purposes.

Example:

- **T5** treats multiple tasks as text-to-text problems, where the model learns to perform a variety of NLP tasks (such as translation, summarization, and classification) using a unified framework.

3. Visualizing the Pre-Training Process

Training Objective and Data Flow:

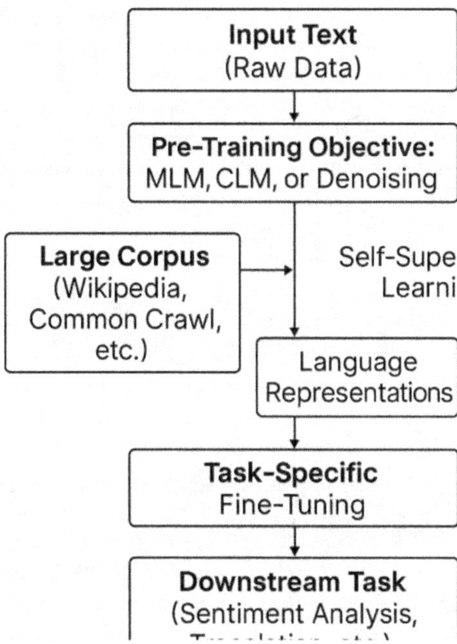

In the diagram:

- **Pre-training** starts with raw input text, where self-supervised learning is used to create rich language representations.

- The model learns through **masking** (MLM), predicting **next-word** (CLM), or **reconstructing** missing text (Denoising Autoencoding).

- The resulting language representations are then fine-tuned for specific tasks, allowing the model to perform effectively on downstream applications.

4. Challenges in Pre-Training Large Language Models

a) **High Computational Cost**: Pre-training large language models requires significant computational resources, including GPUs or TPUs, large-scale storage, and high energy consumption.

b) **Environmental Impact**: Training large-scale models contributes to the environmental footprint due to the high energy consumption required for training on massive datasets.

c) **Data Bias and Ethical Concerns**: Pre-training models on large text corpora that include biased content can lead to models inheriting those biases. Addressing bias in pre-trained models remains an important challenge in NLP.

d) **Memory and Storage Requirements**: Large language models require substantial memory and storage during both training and inference. This makes them challenging to deploy in resource-constrained environments.

Pre-training large language models is a crucial step in building powerful, generalizable NLP systems. By learning from vast amounts of unannotated text data, models can develop rich language representations that can be fine-tuned for a wide variety of downstream tasks. The methods and strategies involved in pre-training, including **masked language modeling (MLM), causal language modeling (CLM), denoising autoencoding**, and **multi-task pre-training**, have paved the way for breakthroughs in NLP.

While the pre-training phase is resource-intensive and comes with challenges like computational costs and ethical concerns, its benefits in enabling transfer learning, improving task performance, and making models more adaptable to a wide range of tasks have made it an indispensable approach in modern NLP. As the field continues to evolve, pre-training techniques will likely become even more efficient and adaptable, further driving advancements in language understanding and AI systems.

Popular Pre-Trained Models

Large language models (LLMs) have become the cornerstone of modern Natural Language Processing (NLP), enabling state-of-the-art performance across a wide range of tasks, including text classification, translation, summarization, question answering, and text generation. A key aspect of the success of LLMs is **pre-training**, a phase in which models are trained on massive amounts of unannotated text data to learn general language representations. Once pre-trained, these models can then be **fine-tuned** for specific tasks with smaller, task-specific datasets.

Since the introduction of the transformer model in 2017, several notable pre-trained models like **BERT**, **GPT**, **T5**, and **RoBERTa** have set new benchmarks in NLP. These models differ in their architecture, training objectives, and areas of application.

1. BERT (Bidirectional Encoder Representations from Transformers)

Overview of BERT

BERT, introduced by Google in 2018, was one of the first models to leverage a **bidirectional attention mechanism** for NLP. Prior to BERT, models like GPT used unidirectional (left-to-right) attention. BERT's bidirectional attention allows it to better understand the context of words, which significantly improved performance on a wide range of NLP tasks.

Key Features of BERT:

a) **Bidirectional Contextualization**: BERT learns to understand context by looking at the surrounding words (both left and right) of any given word in a sentence. This is crucial for handling polysemy (words with multiple meanings), where the meaning of a word depends on its surrounding words.

b) **Masked Language Modeling (MLM)**: During pre-training, BERT uses **masked language modeling**, where a random selection of words in the input sequence is replaced by a **[MASK]** token. The model is then trained to predict the original words based on the surrounding context. This allows BERT to learn deep contextual relationships between words in a sentence.

c) **Next-Sentence Prediction (NSP)**: BERT also learns relationships between consecutive sentences by predicting whether a second sentence logically follows the first one. This task helps the model understand sentence-level discourse and context.

Training Procedure for BERT:

- **Pre-training**: BERT is pre-trained on a large corpus like **Wikipedia** and **BooksCorpus** using the MLM and NSP tasks.
- **Fine-tuning**: After pre-training, BERT can be fine-tuned for specific downstream tasks like **question answering** (SQuAD), **sentiment analysis**, and **named entity recognition** (NER).

Applications of BERT:

- **Text Classification**: BERT excels at tasks like sentiment analysis, where it classifies text into categories like positive or negative.
- **Question Answering**: BERT is fine-tuned on datasets like SQuAD to answer open-domain questions based on a passage of text.
- **Named Entity Recognition (NER)**: BERT is used to identify entities such as people, organizations, and locations in text.

Graphical Representation of BERT:

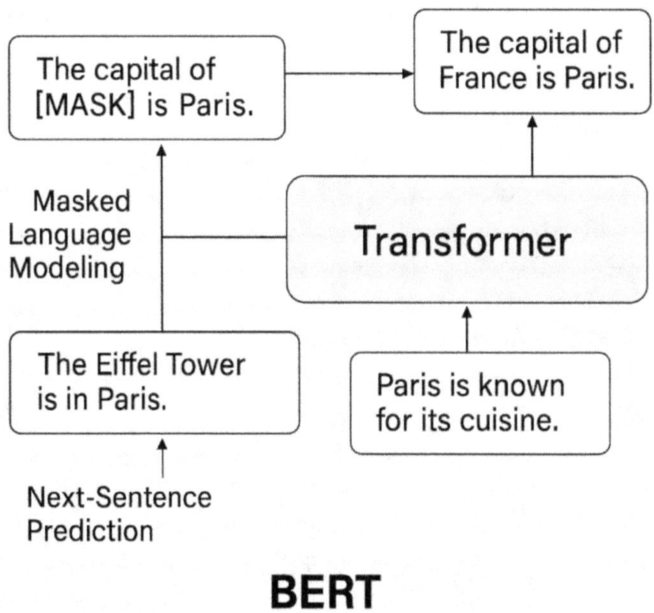

In this diagram, BERT uses both masked language modeling and next-sentence prediction during pre-training to understand the context of words and their relationships across sentences.

2. GPT (Generative Pre-trained Transformer)

Overview of GPT

GPT (Generative Pre-trained Transformer), developed by OpenAI, is an autoregressive transformer model designed for **text generation**. Unlike BERT, which is trained bidirectionally, GPT uses a **unidirectional** (left-to-right) attention mechanism, meaning it predicts the next word based on the previous context in the sequence. GPT has undergone several versions, with **GPT-3** being one of the largest models, containing 175 billion parameters.

Key Features of GPT:

a) **Unidirectional Attention**: GPT is trained with **causal language modeling**, where the model predicts the next word in the sequence based on the words that have come before it. This unidirectional approach makes it ideal for generative tasks where the model creates coherent text one word at a time.

b) **Pre-training Objective**: GPT is pre-trained on a large corpus using an **autoregressive** objective, where it learns to predict the next word in a sequence given the previous words.

c) **Fine-Tuning**: After pre-training, GPT can be fine-tuned on specific tasks such as text completion, summarization, translation, and even more creative applications like poetry generation.

Training Procedure for GPT:

- **Pre-training**: GPT is pre-trained on a large corpus like **Common Crawl**, **BooksCorpus**, and other text datasets.
- **Fine-tuning**: After pre-training, GPT is fine-tuned on specific downstream tasks, often using much smaller labeled datasets.

Applications of GPT:

- **Text Generation**: GPT is widely used for generating coherent and contextually relevant text for applications like chatbots, content creation, and story generation.
- **Text Completion**: GPT can complete sentences or paragraphs based on a prompt.
- **Summarization**: GPT can be fine-tuned for abstractive summarization, generating concise summaries of long documents.

Graphical Representation of GPT:

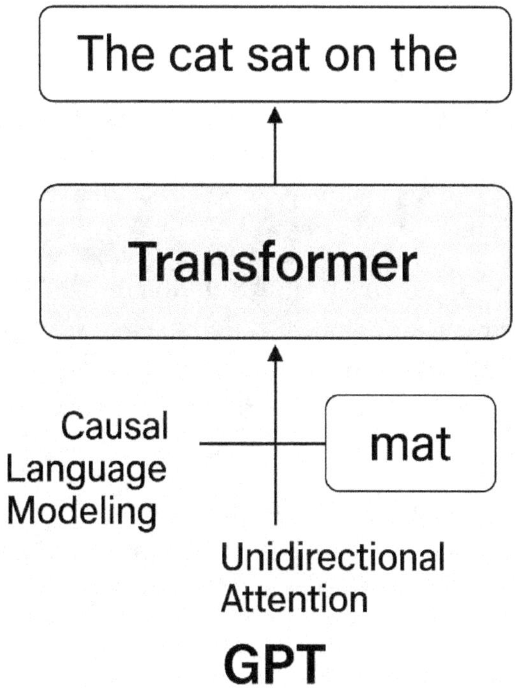

In the diagram, GPT uses a causal language modeling objective with unidirectional attention to predict the next word in a sequence, making it suitable for text generation tasks.

3. T5 (Text-to-Text Transfer Transformer)

Overview of T5

T5, developed by Google, takes a novel approach by framing all NLP tasks as **text-to-text problems**. This means that for any task (such as translation, summarization, or question answering), both the input and output are treated as text sequences. T5 was trained on a large-scale, multi-task learning setup, where the model learned to handle a variety of NLP tasks by converting them into a text generation problem.

Key Features of T5:

a) **Unified Text-to-Text Framework**: T5 simplifies the task-specific approach by using the same architecture for all tasks. For example, a translation task is framed as "translate English to French: [text]," and a summarization task is framed as "summarize: [text]."

b) **Pre-training Objective**: T5 uses a **denoising autoencoding** objective, where random portions of the input text are masked or corrupted, and the model is tasked with reconstructing the original, uncorrupted text. This enables T5 to learn representations that generalize well across a wide variety of tasks.

c) **Multitask Pre-training**: T5 was pre-trained on a mixture of tasks, including text classification, translation, summarization, and question answering, allowing the model to generalize better to new tasks.

Training Procedure for T5:

- **Pre-training**: T5 was pre-trained using the **Colossal Clean Crawled Corpus (C4)** and other datasets, learning to generate the target text from a corrupted or masked version of the input.
- **Fine-tuning**: After pre-training, T5 can be fine-tuned on specific downstream tasks using smaller, task-specific datasets.

Applications of T5:

- **Text Translation**: T5 can translate text from one language to another by framing the task as a text-to-text problem.
- **Text Summarization**: T5 can summarize long documents by generating a concise summary from the input text.

- **Question Answering**: T5 can answer questions based on a given passage of text by generating a response as a text sequence.

Graphical Representation of T5:

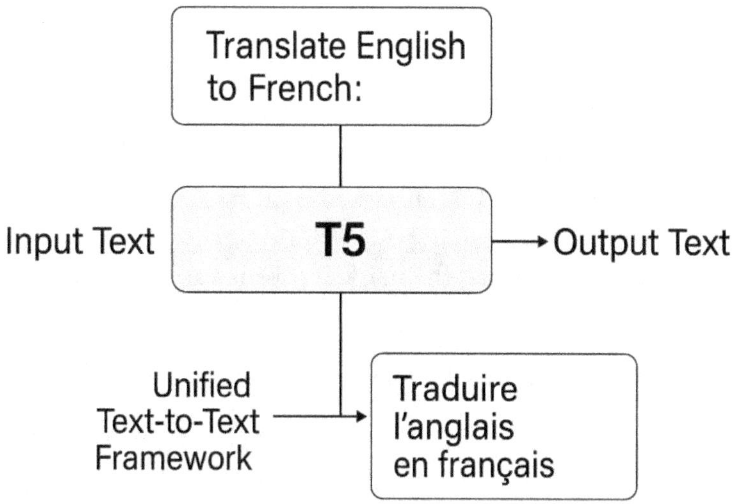

In this diagram, T5 uses a unified text-to-text framework, where every NLP task is treated as a problem of converting one text sequence into another.

4. RoBERTa (Robustly Optimized BERT Pretraining Approach)

Overview of RoBERTa

RoBERTa is an optimized variant of **BERT**, developed by Facebook AI. RoBERTa seeks to improve on BERT's pre-training procedure by exploring different hyperparameters, training on larger datasets, and removing the **next-sentence prediction (NSP)** task that BERT used. RoBERTa has shown that more data, longer training times, and better hyperparameters can lead to significant improvements in model performance.

Key Features of RoBERTa:

a) **Removal of Next-Sentence Prediction (NSP)**: RoBERTa removes the next-sentence prediction task, which was part of BERT's pre-training. Research found that NSP contributed little to the performance of the model.

b) **Larger Training Data**: RoBERTa was trained on a much larger dataset (160GB of text data) than BERT, which improved its generalization and performance on downstream tasks.

c) **Dynamic Masking**: In contrast to BERT, which uses fixed masking during pre-training, RoBERTa uses **dynamic masking**, meaning that the masked tokens vary every time the model sees the same training example.

Training Procedure for RoBERTa:

- **Pre-training**: RoBERTa was trained using a large dataset and a more aggressive training schedule.
- **Fine-tuning**: After pre-training, RoBERTa is fine-tuned on task-specific datasets, similar to BERT.

Applications of RoBERTa:

- **Text Classification**: RoBERTa can be used for classifying text into categories, such as spam detection or sentiment analysis.
- **Question Answering**: RoBERTa is fine-tuned on question-answering datasets like SQuAD to answer open-domain questions based on a passage of text.
- **Named Entity Recognition (NER)**: RoBERTa can be used to identify named entities in text.

5. DistilBERT

Overview of DistilBERT

DistilBERT is a smaller and faster version of **BERT**, created through a technique called **knowledge distillation**. The goal of DistilBERT is to reduce the size and computational cost of BERT while retaining most of its performance, making it suitable for deployment in resource-constrained environments.

Key Features of DistilBERT:

a) **Knowledge Distillation**: DistilBERT is trained using a **teacher-student** paradigm, where the "student" model (DistilBERT) learns to mimic the behavior of the larger "teacher" model (BERT).

b) **Smaller and Faster**: DistilBERT is 60% smaller and 60% faster than BERT, making it more efficient while retaining 97% of BERT's performance on downstream tasks.

Training Procedure for DistilBERT:

- **Pre-training**: DistilBERT is pre-trained using the same dataset as BERT, but with fewer parameters.

- **Fine-tuning**: After pre-training, DistilBERT can be fine-tuned on specific NLP tasks, just like BERT.

Applications of DistilBERT:

- **Text Classification**: DistilBERT can be used for tasks like sentiment analysis and document classification with fewer computational resources.

- **Named Entity Recognition**: DistilBERT can be used for identifying entities in text, such as organizations and locations.

Conclusion

Pre-trained large language models, such as **BERT**, **GPT**, **T5**, **RoBERTa**, and **DistilBERT**, have dramatically advanced the field of NLP. Each model offers unique innovations in terms of architecture, pre-training objectives, and application domains. BERT's bidirectional attention, GPT's unidirectional autoregressive modeling, T5's unified text-to-text framework, RoBERTa's optimization of BERT's training process, and DistilBERT's knowledge distillation have all contributed to improving the performance and efficiency of NLP systems.

As the demand for more efficient and adaptable NLP models grows, these pre-trained models will continue to serve as the backbone for a wide range of applications, from language understanding and generation to question answering and machine translation. With ongoing research, the landscape of pre-trained models is expected to evolve, incorporating new techniques for making models more efficient, ethical, and robust.

Chapter 7: Fine-Tuning LLMs for Specific Tasks

Concept of Fine-Tuning

In the field of Natural Language Processing (NLP), large language models (LLMs) like **BERT**, **GPT**, **T5**, and **RoBERTa** have achieved significant breakthroughs by learning vast general language representations during the **pre-training** phase. However, despite their impressive generalization capabilities, these pre-trained models are not immediately optimal for specific tasks such as **sentiment analysis, named entity recognition (NER), machine translation**, or **question answering**. This is where **fine-tuning** comes into play.

Fine-tuning is a transfer learning technique that enables pre-trained LLMs to be specialized for specific tasks by training them on smaller, task-specific labeled datasets. Fine-tuning allows LLMs to adjust their general language knowledge to meet the demands of particular applications, enhancing the model's performance on these tasks while leveraging the knowledge it gained during pre-training.

1. What is Fine-Tuning?

Fine-tuning is the process of **adapting a pre-trained model** to perform a specific task. During pre-training, the model learns general language representations from a large, unannotated corpus of text (e.g., Wikipedia, books, Common Crawl). However, these representations are not fully optimized for any single NLP task. Fine-tuning involves training the model on labeled data specific to the task at hand, allowing it to adjust its parameters to optimize performance for that particular task.

In the fine-tuning process, the model retains the general language understanding it gained during pre-training but **refines** its parameters using the smaller, labeled dataset for the target task. This results in a model that performs well not only on language understanding but also on specific application tasks.

Key Differences Between Pre-Training and Fine-Tuning:

- **Pre-Training**: The model is trained on large, unannotated corpora to learn general language patterns and structures.
- **Fine-Tuning**: The model is adapted to a specific downstream task by training it on a smaller, labeled dataset, allowing it to specialize in the task's specific needs.

2. The Fine-Tuning Process

Fine-tuning an LLM for a specific task typically follows these steps:

a) Load Pre-Trained Model

The first step in fine-tuning is to load a pre-trained model that has already learned general language representations. Popular pre-trained models include:

- **BERT** (Bidirectional Encoder Representations from Transformers)
- **GPT** (Generative Pre-trained Transformer)
- **T5** (Text-to-Text Transfer Transformer)
- **RoBERTa** (Robustly Optimized BERT Pretraining Approach)

These models are trained on large text corpora and have learned to capture a wide range of language features, such as grammar, syntax, semantics, and even certain factual knowledge.

b) Prepare Task-Specific Dataset

Once the pre-trained model is loaded, the next step is to prepare the task-specific dataset. This dataset contains labeled examples of the task that the model needs to perform. The dataset could vary depending on the task, such as:

- **For Text Classification**: Labeled data where each text sample is assigned to a specific class (e.g., positive or negative sentiment).
- **For Named Entity Recognition (NER)**: Labeled data that marks named entities (such as organizations, locations, and people) in the text.
- **For Question Answering**: A dataset where each question is paired with an answer from a given passage.

The task-specific dataset is often much smaller than the data used for pre-training, but it is crucial for fine-tuning the model for specialized tasks.

c) Modify the Model for the Task

Fine-tuning usually involves adjusting the output layer of the model to match the specific requirements of the task. For example:

- For **classification tasks**, the model's final layer is replaced with a **softmax layer** that outputs probabilities for each class.
- For **question answering tasks**, the final layer can be modified to output start and end positions for the answer span within the context passage.

In many cases, only the output layer and a few of the intermediate layers are modified, leaving most of the model's architecture (such as the self-attention layers) unchanged. This allows the model to leverage its pre-trained language knowledge while adapting to the specific task.

d) Train the Model (Fine-Tuning)

During fine-tuning, the pre-trained model is trained on the task-specific dataset using supervised learning. The model's parameters are updated based on the labeled data, with the objective of minimizing a **task-specific loss function** (e.g., cross-entropy loss for classification tasks). Fine-tuning typically requires much fewer epochs and data than pre-training due to the model's prior knowledge.

Fine-tuning is done using gradient-based optimization algorithms like **Adam** or **SGD**, which adjust the model's weights to reduce the error in predictions.

e) Evaluate and Optimize

After fine-tuning, the model's performance is evaluated on a separate **validation set** that was not seen during training. This helps ensure that the model is generalizing well to new data and not overfitting to the training data. Hyperparameters (such as the learning rate, batch size, and number of fine-tuning epochs) may be adjusted based on the validation performance to further optimize the model.

3. Why is Fine-Tuning Important?

Fine-tuning plays a pivotal role in improving the performance of large language models by adapting them to the nuances of specific tasks. Below are the key reasons why fine-tuning is so important:

a) Specialized Performance

Pre-trained models, although powerful, are not optimized for specific tasks. Fine-tuning tailors the model to perform better on tasks like **question answering**, **sentiment analysis**, or **text summarization**, improving accuracy and efficiency.

For example, a general language model might have trouble distinguishing between positive and negative sentiment in a text. However, by fine-tuning it on a labeled sentiment dataset, the model becomes more adept at classifying sentiments based on the specific language patterns seen in the task.

b) Transfer Learning

Fine-tuning allows LLMs to benefit from **transfer learning**, where the knowledge acquired during pre-training on a large corpus is transferred to specialized tasks. This allows models to achieve impressive performance on downstream tasks with relatively small amounts of labeled data. Fine-tuning effectively **bridges the gap** between the general knowledge learned during pre-training and the task-specific knowledge required for real-world applications.

c) Reduced Training Time and Data Requirements

Fine-tuning is much faster and requires less data compared to training a model from scratch. Pre-trained models, such as BERT or GPT, have already learned general language features, so fine-tuning focuses on task-specific adjustments. This significantly reduces the training time and the amount of labeled data needed for achieving good performance.

d) Generalization to New Tasks

Fine-tuned models are highly adaptable and can generalize well to new tasks, even if they are somewhat different from the ones they were pre-trained on. For example, a BERT model pre-trained on general text data can be fine-tuned for a medical text classification task, where it learns domain-specific language while retaining the general linguistic knowledge.

4. Benefits of Fine-Tuning Pre-Trained Models

Fine-tuning pre-trained large language models offers several practical benefits, especially for NLP tasks that require quick deployment and high accuracy.

a) Accessibility to Non-Experts

Fine-tuning makes it possible for researchers and practitioners with limited resources or expertise in deep learning to leverage powerful pre-trained models. By focusing on fine-tuning, researchers can apply cutting-edge NLP techniques without needing to develop models from scratch or invest heavily in large-scale computational resources.

b) Flexibility in NLP Applications

Fine-tuning allows the same pre-trained model to be applied to a wide variety of tasks. Since the underlying architecture remains the same, the same model can be adapted for tasks ranging from **text classification** and **entity recognition** to more complex tasks like **dialog systems** or **document generation**.

c) Enhanced Performance with Task-Specific Data

Fine-tuning allows the model to learn task-specific features that are essential for high performance. For example, fine-tuning on a **question answering** dataset like **SQuAD** enables the model to become highly skilled at answering open-ended questions based on a passage of text.

5. Practical Example of Fine-Tuning with BERT

Let's walk through a practical example of fine-tuning **BERT** for a **sentiment analysis** task.

Step 1: Pre-Trained Model

We start with the pre-trained **BERT-base** model, which has been trained on a large corpus such as **Wikipedia** and **BooksCorpus**. This model has learned general language patterns and is ready to be fine-tuned.

Step 2: Dataset Preparation

We prepare a labeled dataset of movie reviews, where each review is labeled as either positive or negative sentiment. For example:

- Review: "This movie was fantastic!" -> Label: Positive
- Review: "It was a waste of time." -> Label: Negative

Step 3: Model Modification

We replace BERT's output layer with a **softmax layer** to predict two classes: Positive or Negative sentiment.

Step 4: Fine-Tuning

We fine-tune the model using the labeled dataset. The training involves updating the model's weights using the labeled data to minimize the error between the predicted sentiment and the actual label.

Step 5: Evaluation

After fine-tuning, we evaluate the model's performance on a separate validation set of movie reviews. The accuracy, precision, and recall metrics are calculated to assess the model's sentiment classification ability.

6. Challenges in Fine-Tuning

While fine-tuning pre-trained models is highly effective, it is not without its challenges:

1. **Overfitting**: Fine-tuning on small datasets can lead to overfitting, where the model learns to perform very well on the training data but fails to generalize to unseen data.
2. **Domain Adaptation**: When fine-tuning on domain-specific tasks (e.g., medical text), the pre-trained model may need more specialized fine-tuning to handle domain-specific vocabulary and jargon effectively.
3. **Hyperparameter Tuning**: Fine-tuning often requires careful tuning of hyperparameters (such as learning rate, batch size, and number of epochs) to achieve optimal results. This process can be time-consuming and computationally expensive.

Fine-tuning large language models is an essential step in adapting pre-trained models for specialized NLP tasks. By leveraging the general language knowledge learned during pre-training, fine-tuning allows models to perform well on specific applications with minimal task-specific data. Fine-tuning makes advanced NLP techniques more accessible and efficient, improving performance on a wide variety of tasks, from sentiment analysis and named entity recognition to complex language generation tasks.

Despite the challenges involved, fine-tuning continues to be the most practical and effective way to apply the power of pre-trained large language models to real-world problems in NLP. As the field continues to evolve, fine-tuning will remain a core strategy for optimizing the performance of NLP systems.

Steps for Fine-Tuning

Fine-tuning is a crucial process for adapting large pre-trained language models (LLMs) to specific Natural Language Processing (NLP) tasks. Pre-trained models like **BERT**, **GPT**, **T5**, and **RoBERTa** have been trained on massive corpora and have learned generalized language representations. However, to apply them to specialized tasks such as **sentiment analysis**, **named entity recognition (NER)**, or **question answering (QA)**, fine-tuning is necessary. This process involves training a pre-trained model on a task-specific labeled dataset to make it more efficient and accurate for a given task.

In this section, we will discuss the **steps for fine-tuning** large language models, from preparing the data and modifying the model architecture to training and evaluating the model. We will also look at some of the practical aspects and challenges that arise during the fine-tuning process.

1. Step 1: Choose a Pre-Trained Model

Before fine-tuning a model for a specific task, it's essential to select an appropriate **pre-trained model**. The choice of model depends on the nature of the task, available resources, and desired performance. Some popular pre-trained models include:

- **BERT**: Best suited for tasks that require understanding bidirectional context, such as **text classification**, **NER**, and **question answering**.
- **GPT**: Ideal for tasks requiring **text generation**, such as **creative writing** and **dialog systems**.
- **T5**: Useful for **text-to-text tasks**, such as **summarization**, **translation**, and **paraphrasing**.
- **RoBERTa**: A robust variant of BERT, designed to perform better on downstream tasks by optimizing pre-training strategies.

2. Step 2: Prepare the Task-Specific Dataset

Once the pre-trained model has been chosen, the next step is to **prepare the dataset** specific to the task. A task-specific dataset consists of labeled data that aligns with the objective of the NLP task you are aiming to solve.

Preparing the Dataset:

- **Text Classification (e.g., Sentiment Analysis)**: For classification tasks, the dataset typically consists of sentences or documents with corresponding labels (e.g., "positive" or "negative" sentiment).

Example:

  - Input Text: "This movie was amazing!"
  - Label: Positive

- **Named Entity Recognition (NER)**: For NER tasks, the dataset contains sentences where named entities (like names of people, organizations, or locations) are annotated.

Example:

  - Input Text: "Barack Obama was born in Hawaii."
  - Label: "Barack Obama" (Person), "Hawaii" (Location)

- **Question Answering**: For QA tasks, the dataset includes a passage of text, a question, and the corresponding answer.

Example:

  - Passage: "The capital of France is Paris."
  - Question: "What is the capital of France?"
  - Answer: "Paris"

- **Text Generation**: For generation tasks, the dataset typically includes prompt-output pairs (e.g., machine translation, text summarization).

Example:

  - Input: "Translate English to French: How are you?"
  - Output: "Comment ça va ?"

Data Preprocessing:

- **Tokenization**: The dataset needs to be tokenized into subwords or words, depending on the tokenizer used in the pre-trained model (e.g., WordPiece for BERT, Byte-Pair Encoding for GPT).
- **Padding**: Input sequences are typically padded to a fixed length to ensure uniformity across batches.

- **Label Encoding**: In classification tasks, labels need to be encoded into numerical format (e.g., "positive" = 1, "negative" = 0).

3. Step 3: Modify the Model Architecture for the Task

After preparing the dataset, the next step is to modify the model's architecture to fit the specific task. This usually involves adding or adjusting the final output layer.

Task-Specific Modifications:

- **Text Classification**: Replace the original output layer with a **softmax** layer for multi-class classification or a **sigmoid** layer for binary classification.

Example: In BERT for sentiment analysis, the final layer is replaced with a classifier that outputs a sentiment label (e.g., positive or negative).

- **Named Entity Recognition (NER)**: For NER, replace the final layer with one that outputs labels for each token in the input sequence. This is typically done using a **CRF (Conditional Random Field)** or **softmax** over tokens.

Example: BERT's output will be a sequence of labels such as "Person" for "Barack Obama" and "Location" for "Hawaii".

- **Question Answering**: Modify the model to output **start** and **end** positions for the answer span in the passage.

Example: For SQuAD-style question answering, the model is fine-tuned to predict the start and end positions of the answer in the text.

- **Text Generation**: If fine-tuning for text generation, the model's output layer remains largely the same, but it is trained with **autoregressive** objectives to predict the next token in the sequence.

Graphical Representation of Model Modification for Text Classification:

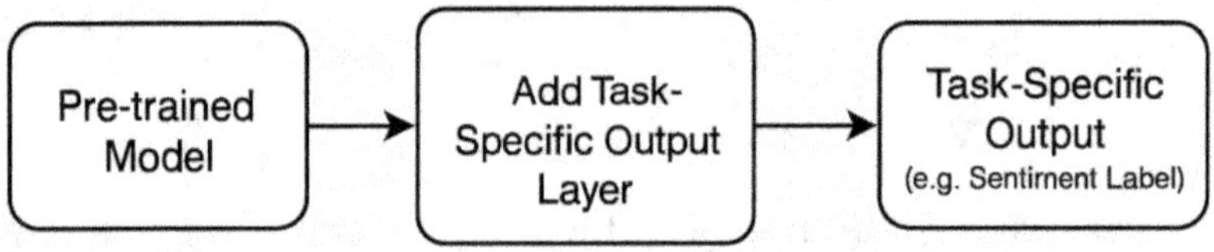

In the diagram, the pre-trained model is adapted for a specific task (e.g., sentiment analysis) by adding a task-specific output layer.

4. Step 4: Fine-Tuning the Model

Fine-tuning involves training the model on the task-specific dataset, allowing the pre-trained model to adjust its parameters to perform better on the new task.

Training Procedure:

1. **Load the Pre-Trained Model**: Load the pre-trained model and its tokenizer, ensuring it is ready for fine-tuning.
2. **Set Training Hyperparameters**: Choose hyperparameters like learning rate, batch size, number of epochs, etc. Fine-tuning typically requires a smaller learning rate because the model has

already learned general language representations during pre-training.

3. **Optimization**: Use an optimizer (e.g., **Adam** or **AdamW**) to minimize the loss function. For text classification, this could be **cross-entropy loss**, while for QA, the loss might be based on the difference between the predicted answer spans and the actual spans.
4. **Early Stopping**: Implement **early stopping** to prevent overfitting and save the best model.
5. **Monitor Metrics**: During training, track the model's performance on validation data using metrics such as **accuracy**, **F1 score**, or **mean average precision (mAP)** for classification tasks.

Graphical Representation of Fine-Tuning:

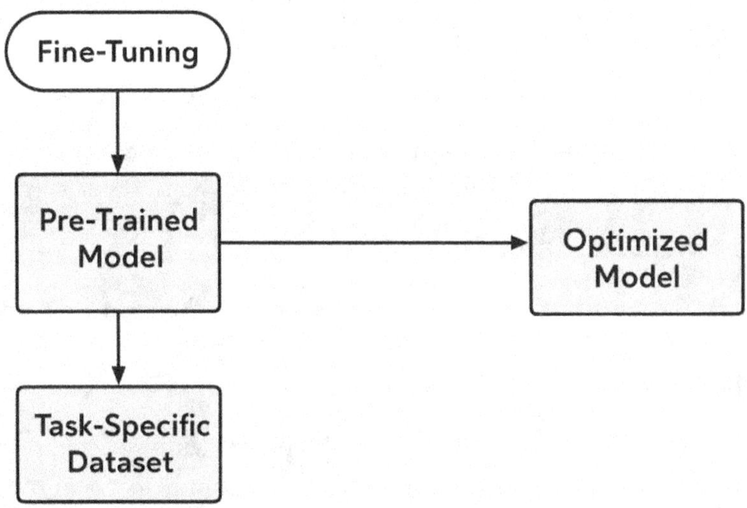

In this diagram, the pre-trained model undergoes fine-tuning on the task-specific dataset, resulting in an optimized model for the particular task.

5. Step 5: Evaluate the Model's Performance

After fine-tuning, the model needs to be evaluated on a **validation or test dataset** to assess its performance and generalization capability.

Evaluation Metrics:

- **Accuracy**: The proportion of correctly classified instances.
- **Precision**: The proportion of true positives among all positive predictions.
- **Recall**: The proportion of true positives among all actual positives.
- **F1 Score**: The harmonic mean of precision and recall, used when there is an imbalance between classes.
- **BLEU Score** (for generation tasks): Measures the overlap between the model-generated text and reference text.
- **ROUGE Score** (for summarization tasks): Measures the overlap of n-grams between the model's output and a reference summary.

Post-Evaluation Optimization:

- **Hyperparameter Tuning**: After evaluating the model, additional hyperparameter tuning may be required to further improve performance.
- **Model Calibration**: Fine-tuning the model with more data or using techniques like **data augmentation** can help boost the model's generalization ability.

Graphical Representation of Evaluation:

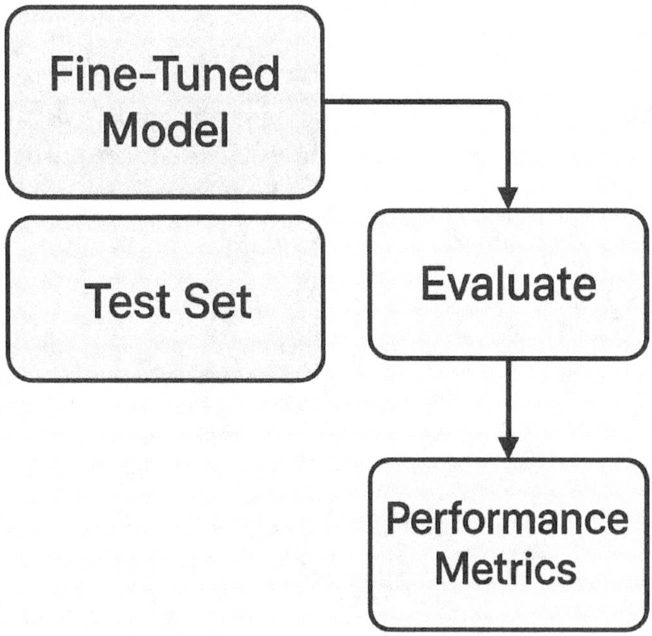

In this diagram, the fine-tuned model is evaluated on a test set, and performance metrics are calculated to analyze its effectiveness.

6. Step 6: Deploy the Model for Real-World Use

Once the model has been fine-tuned and evaluated, it is ready for deployment. The deployment process involves integrating the model into an application or system where it can make predictions on new, unseen data.

Deployment Considerations:

- **Model Size**: Fine-tuned models, especially large ones, may need to be compressed or optimized for faster inference and lower memory usage (e.g., using techniques like **quantization** or **pruning**).

- **Scalability**: Ensure the model is scalable for real-time predictions or batch processing, depending on the use case.
- **Monitoring**: Continuously monitor the model's performance in production to identify issues such as **concept drift** (changes in the input data distribution over time) and retrain the model periodically as needed.

Graphical Representation of Deployment:

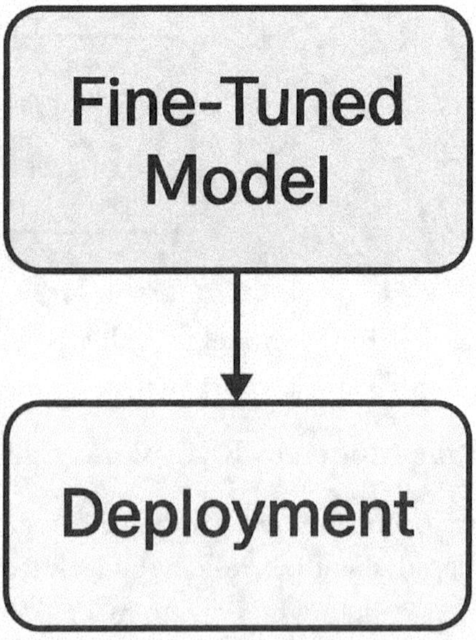

In the diagram, the fine-tuned model is deployed for real-time or batch predictions in production environments.

7. Challenges in Fine-Tuning LLMs

Fine-tuning large language models comes with several challenges:

1. **Overfitting**: Fine-tuning on small datasets can cause the model to memorize the training data rather than generalizing to unseen examples.
2. **Computational Resources**: Fine-tuning large models requires significant computational power, particularly when working with very large datasets or models (e.g., GPT-3).
3. **Data Quality**: The performance of the fine-tuned model depends heavily on the quality of the task-specific dataset. Poorly labeled data can degrade model performance.
4. **Biases in Data**: LLMs may inherit biases from the pre-trained corpus and task-specific datasets, which can lead to biased predictions.

Fine-tuning is a critical process that enables pre-trained large language models to perform well on specific NLP tasks. By leveraging the general knowledge learned during pre-training and adapting it to task-specific datasets, fine-tuning allows models to perform effectively on tasks such as sentiment analysis, named entity recognition, and question answering.

The steps for fine-tuning - from choosing the right model and preparing the dataset to modifying the architecture and evaluating the performance - provide a structured approach for improving task-specific performance. While there are challenges to fine-tuning, including computational costs and the risk of overfitting, the benefits of fine-tuning make it a vital part of deploying LLMs for real-world applications.

Practical Case Studies

Introduction

Fine-tuning large language models (LLMs) for specific tasks has become a fundamental strategy in achieving high-performance results across a wide variety of applications in Natural Language Processing (NLP). Models such as **BERT**, **GPT**, **T5**, and **RoBERTa** provide general-purpose language understanding capabilities after pre-training on large corpora of text. However, to apply these models to specialized tasks—such as **sentiment analysis**, **named entity recognition (NER)**, or **question answering**—fine-tuning is necessary. Fine-tuning adjusts these models to perform optimally on task-specific datasets.

1. Case Study 1: Fine-Tuning BERT for Sentiment Analysis

Background:

Sentiment analysis involves determining the sentiment (positive, negative, or neutral) expressed in a piece of text. This task is widely used in social media monitoring, customer feedback analysis, and brand sentiment tracking. **BERT** has been successfully fine-tuned for sentiment analysis tasks due to its bidirectional understanding of context.

Fine-Tuning Process:

1. **Pre-Trained Model**: Start with a **pre-trained BERT** model that has been trained on large corpora such as Wikipedia and BooksCorpus.
2. **Task-Specific Dataset**: Use a labeled dataset of text samples annotated with sentiment labels (e.g., positive or negative sentiment). One such dataset is the **IMDb Movie Reviews Dataset**, which contains 50,000 labeled movie reviews.

3. **Modify Model Architecture**: Replace the final layer of BERT with a **softmax layer** that outputs probabilities for the sentiment classes (positive, negative). The output size of this layer matches the number of classes (e.g., 2 for binary sentiment classification).

4. **Fine-Tuning**: Train the model on the sentiment dataset using a supervised learning approach, optimizing for a loss function like **cross-entropy** to minimize the error between predicted and actual labels.

5. **Evaluation**: After fine-tuning, evaluate the model's performance on a held-out test set using metrics like **accuracy**, **precision**, **recall**, and **F1 score**.

Results:

Fine-tuning BERT for sentiment analysis typically results in a high **F1 score** because BERT's bidirectional attention allows it to understand the full context of the text. By leveraging the model's pre-trained knowledge, BERT can accurately classify sentiment, even with complex, nuanced phrases.

Graphical Representation of Sentiment Analysis Fine-Tuning:

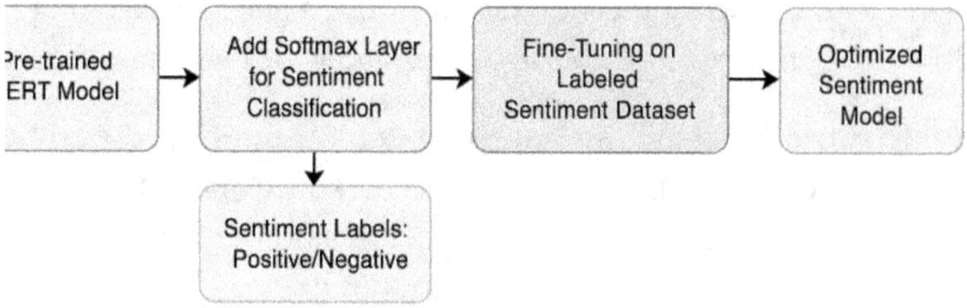

2. Case Study 2: Fine-Tuning GPT for Text Generation

Background:

GPT is widely used for **text generation** tasks such as creative writing, chatbot responses, and automatic story generation. Fine-tuning GPT for generating coherent, contextually relevant text based on a specific prompt has shown remarkable results.

Fine-Tuning Process:

a) **Pre-Trained Model**: Start with a **pre-trained GPT** model, which has been trained on large text corpora like **Common Crawl**. GPT is already skilled in generating coherent text based on previous tokens.

b) **Task-Specific Dataset**: For a creative writing task, use a dataset of text written in a specific style or genre (e.g., science fiction stories). The model will learn the nuances of that genre's writing style during fine-tuning.

c) **Modify Model Architecture**: GPT typically uses the same architecture for both pre-training and fine-tuning, with the main change being the output generated token at each step. No drastic changes are required for the architecture.

d) **Fine-Tuning**: Fine-tune the model using supervised learning on the task-specific dataset. The model learns to generate text that aligns with the writing style present in the dataset, improving its ability to generate similar stories, dialogues, or narratives.

e) **Evaluation**: Evaluate the generated text on **fluency**, **creativity**, and **coherence**. Metrics such as **BLEU score** and **ROUGE score** can be used to measure the quality and overlap of n-grams between the generated text and the reference text.

Results:

Fine-tuning GPT for a specific genre or writing style significantly improves the quality and relevance of generated text. For example, fine-tuning on a **science fiction** dataset will result in the model generating more contextually relevant and coherent science fiction stories.

Graphical Representation of GPT Fine-Tuning for Text Generation:

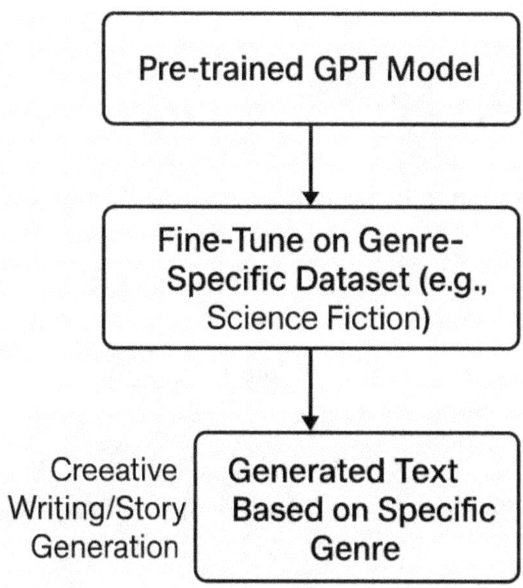

3. Case Study 3: Fine-Tuning BERT for Named Entity Recognition (NER)

Background:

Named Entity Recognition (NER) is a task that involves identifying entities such as **names of people**, **locations**, **organizations**, and other specific terms in text. **BERT** has been successfully fine-tuned for NER tasks, where it learns to classify tokens into predefined categories.

Fine-Tuning Process:

a) **Pre-Trained Model**: Use a **pre-trained BERT model** trained on general language data (like Wikipedia).

b) **Task-Specific Dataset**: Use a labeled dataset that annotates named entities in text. For instance, the **CoNLL-2003** dataset contains labeled NER annotations for English text, with categories like **PERSON, LOCATION, ORGANIZATION,** and **MISC**.

c) **Modify Model Architecture**: Replace the output layer of BERT with a **token classification layer**, where each token is classified into one of the NER categories (or **O** for "no entity").

d) **Fine-Tuning**: Train the model on the NER dataset. During fine-tuning, the model learns to classify each word in the sentence into its corresponding category (e.g., a word like "Barack" would be classified as **PERSON**).

e) **Evaluation**: After fine-tuning, evaluate the model on a held-out test set. Common metrics for NER evaluation include **precision, recall**, and **F1 score**, where a balance between precision and recall is critical for optimal NER performance.

Results:

Fine-tuning BERT for NER tasks leads to impressive performance, as BERT's deep understanding of context allows it to correctly classify named entities even in complex sentences.

Graphical Representation of BERT Fine-Tuning for NER:

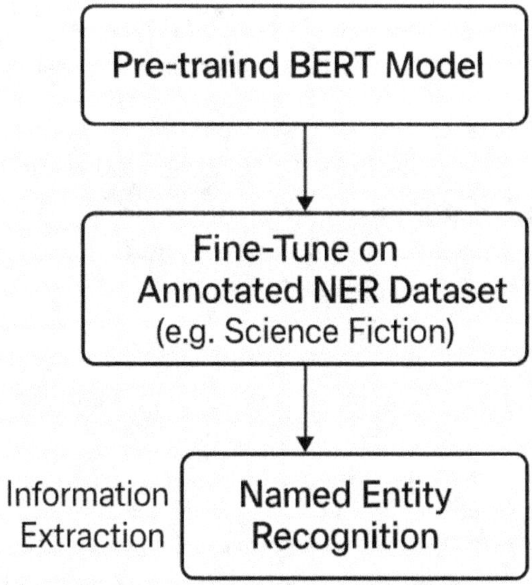

4. Case Study 4: Fine-Tuning T5 for Text Summarization

Background:

Text summarization involves generating a shorter version of a given text while retaining its core information. **T5**, with its **text-to-text framework**, is well-suited for summarization tasks, as it can convert the task into a problem of transforming an input text into a summary.

Fine-Tuning Process:

a) **Pre-Trained Model**: Start with a **pre-trained T5 model**, which has been trained on a large-scale dataset like the **C4** corpus.

b) **Task-Specific Dataset**: Use a dataset specifically for summarization tasks, such as the **CNN/Daily Mail** dataset, where the input consists of news articles and the target is a summary of the article.

c) **Modify Model Architecture**: T5's architecture remains unchanged, as it is designed for text-to-text tasks. The input text is transformed into a summary, with the model learning to generate summaries from long documents.

d) **Fine-Tuning**: Fine-tune T5 on the summarization dataset. The model learns to map long input text to shorter summaries by predicting the next token in the sequence during training.

e) **Evaluation**: Evaluate the quality of the generated summaries using metrics like **ROUGE score**, which measures the overlap of n-grams between the model's generated summary and the reference summary.

Results:

Fine-tuning T5 for summarization leads to coherent, contextually relevant summaries that capture the essence of the input text. T5 can be fine-tuned for different types of summarization, including **extractive** and **abstractive** summarization.

Graphical Representation of T5 Fine-Tuning for Summarization:

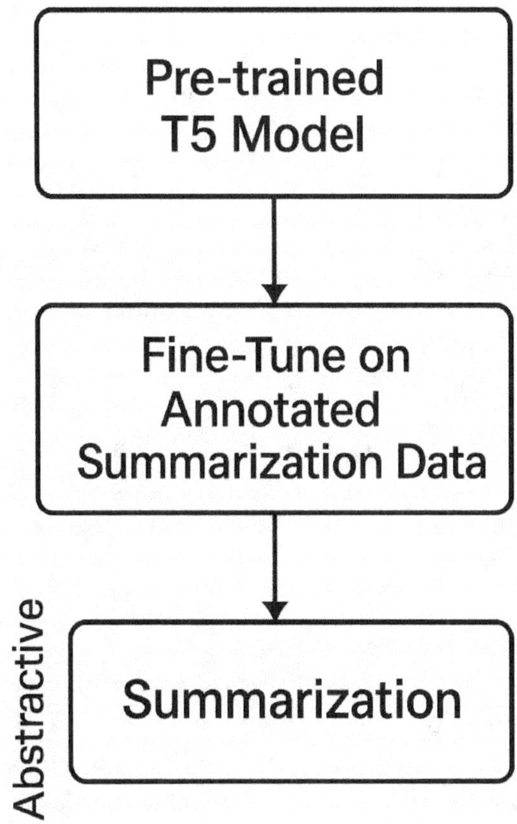

5. Challenges in Fine-Tuning LLMs for Specific Tasks

While fine-tuning is a powerful technique, it does come with several challenges:

a) **Data Scarcity**: Task-specific datasets may be small, leading to overfitting, where the model performs well on training data but poorly on new, unseen data.

b) **Computational Costs**: Fine-tuning large models, especially those like **GPT-3**, requires substantial computational resources, including GPU or TPU usage, which can be cost-prohibitive for some organizations.

c) **Bias in Data**: Pre-trained models, especially those trained on large, diverse datasets, may inherit and amplify biases present in the data. Fine-tuning on biased or unrepresentative task-specific data can exacerbate these issues.

d) **Domain Adaptation**: Fine-tuning for highly specialized domains (e.g., legal or medical text) can be difficult due to domain-specific vocabulary and context. Specialized data is often needed to effectively adapt the model.

Conclusion

Fine-tuning large language models for specific tasks has become a cornerstone of modern NLP, enabling the application of general-purpose pre-trained models like **BERT**, **GPT**, **T5**, and **RoBERTa** to specialized tasks ranging from **sentiment analysis** to **text summarization**. Through practical case studies, we see how fine-tuning allows LLMs to adapt to real-world problems, improving task-specific performance while leveraging the vast language knowledge learned during pre-training.

Despite the challenges involved - such as data scarcity, computational costs, and biases - fine-tuning continues to be an essential technique in deploying powerful NLP systems. As more advanced models and datasets become available, fine-tuning will remain crucial in harnessing the full potential of LLMs for specialized applications in various industries.

Chapter 8: Building Your Own LLM from Scratch

Designing the Architecture

Building a **Large Language Model (LLM)** from scratch is a complex and resource-intensive process that requires a deep understanding of deep learning architectures, optimization techniques, and computational infrastructure. LLMs like **GPT-3**, **BERT**, and **T5** have achieved state-of-the-art performance on a wide variety of Natural Language Processing (NLP) tasks, but creating a model from scratch involves designing an architecture capable of learning general language representations from vast amounts of text data.

The architecture of an LLM is the blueprint that defines how the model processes data, how it learns, and how it generalizes.

1. Understanding the Core Components of LLM Architecture

Designing an LLM starts by understanding the core components that make up the architecture. While the specifics of the architecture may vary depending on the specific task and model, most LLMs follow similar architectural principles, particularly the **transformer architecture**.

a) Embedding Layer

The **embedding layer** is the first layer of the model that converts input text into a numerical representation that the model can process. Each word or token in the text is represented by a high-dimensional vector, and this vector captures the semantic meaning of the word.

- **Tokenization**: The first step is breaking the input text into smaller units (tokens), which could be words, subwords, or characters. The tokenization process depends on the specific model (e.g., WordPiece for BERT or Byte-Pair Encoding for GPT).

- **Word Embeddings**: After tokenization, each token is mapped to an **embedding vector**. These embeddings are learned during pre-training and capture relationships between tokens. Common techniques include **Word2Vec**, **GloVe**, or transformer-based embeddings like **BERT's token embeddings**.

The **embedding layer** is crucial because it initializes the model with basic semantic knowledge about words, which is refined throughout the training process.

b) Transformer Encoder

The **transformer encoder** is the central building block of most modern LLMs. The encoder is responsible for processing the input text and encoding it into contextualized representations. The encoder is composed of multiple layers, each of which contains two main components:

- **Self-Attention Mechanism**: This mechanism allows the model to weigh the importance of each token in the context of the other tokens in the sequence. In **self-attention**, each token attends to every other token in the sequence to capture relationships between them.

- **Feed-Forward Network**: After the self-attention mechanism, the output is passed through a feed-forward neural network to capture complex, non-linear relationships between tokens.

Each layer in the encoder processes the token representations and passes them to the next layer, ultimately generating a rich, contextualized representation of the input text.

c) Transformer Decoder

While many LLMs (such as **BERT**) use only the encoder, some models (like **GPT** and **T5**) also incorporate a **decoder**. The decoder generates the output based on the contextualized representations from the encoder. In the case of **GPT**, the decoder is autoregressive, meaning it predicts the next word in a sequence given the previous context.

- **Causal Self-Attention**: In autoregressive models, the decoder uses **causal self-attention**, which means that each token can only attend to previous tokens, not future ones. This ensures that the model predicts text sequentially, as in text generation tasks.
- **Cross-Attention**: In models like **T5**, the decoder uses **cross-attention** to attend to the encoder's output, enabling the model to generate an output sequence based on the entire input sequence.

d) Positional Encoding

Since transformers process all tokens in parallel, they don't have a built-in notion of token order, unlike RNNs or LSTMs. To address this, **positional encodings** are added to the token embeddings to encode information about the relative or absolute positions of tokens in the sequence.

- **Sinusoidal Positional Encoding**: In **original transformer architectures**, a sinusoidal positional encoding is added to the embeddings to provide a sense of token order.
- **Learnable Positional Encoding**: In some models, positional encodings are treated as learnable parameters that are optimized during training.

Positional encodings allow the model to understand the order of tokens, which is essential for tasks like sentence generation or translation.

2. Key Architectural Decisions for LLM Design

Once the core components are understood, the next step is to make key architectural decisions about the scale and configuration of the model.

a) Number of Layers (Depth)

The number of layers in the **encoder** (and decoder, if applicable) determines the **depth** of the model. Each layer contributes to learning increasingly abstract and complex representations of the input text.

- **Shallow Models**: Fewer layers result in a model that processes information in a simpler manner, capturing only the most basic patterns in the data.
- **Deep Models**: A deeper model can learn more complex relationships, but it also requires more data and computational resources. Very deep models, such as **GPT-3**, have billions of parameters and demand significant computing power to train.

b) Number of Attention Heads

Each **self-attention layer** typically uses multiple attention heads. **Multi-head attention** allows the model to focus on different parts of the sequence simultaneously, learning different types of relationships between tokens.

- **More Heads**: Increasing the number of attention heads allows the model to capture a wider variety of relationships, which can be beneficial for complex tasks such as machine translation or summarization.
- **Performance Trade-offs**: While more attention heads improve model capacity, they also increase computational requirements. The optimal number of heads depends on the size of the model and the available resources.

c) Hidden Size (Width)

The **hidden size** refers to the number of neurons in each layer of the model. A larger hidden size means that the model has more capacity to represent complex information, but it also increases the number of parameters, making the model more computationally expensive.

- **Large Models**: Large hidden sizes allow the model to learn more complex representations but require significantly more memory and processing power.
- **Smaller Models**: Smaller hidden sizes result in fewer parameters, making the model faster and more efficient but potentially limiting its performance on more complex tasks.

d) Model Scaling

One of the critical decisions when designing an LLM is how large the model should be. Model scaling is essential to achieve state-of-the-art performance but also introduces significant computational challenges. Modern LLMs, like **GPT-3** (175 billion parameters), require extensive infrastructure for both training and deployment.

- **Scaling Laws**: Research has shown that larger models generally perform better, but at the cost of increased training time and resources. Fine-tuning a large model can also be more challenging due to its size.
- **Trade-offs**: Designers must balance the model's size with the available computational budget and task requirements. Smaller models may be sufficient for specific tasks and offer better efficiency.

3. Optimization and Training the LLM

Once the architecture is defined, the next step is to optimize and train the LLM. Training a large model involves several key decisions and techniques to ensure efficient learning.

a) Pre-training Objectives

When designing a custom LLM, selecting an appropriate **pre-training objective** is crucial. Some common objectives include:

- **Masked Language Modeling (MLM)**: Used by **BERT**, this objective masks random tokens in the input text and requires the model to predict the missing tokens based on context.
- **Causal Language Modeling**: Used by **GPT**, this autoregressive approach requires the model to predict the next token in the sequence based on previous tokens.
- **Denoising Autoencoding**: Used by models like **T5**, where random parts of the input are corrupted, and the model must reconstruct the original input.

b) Data Preparation and Augmentation

LLMs require vast amounts of data for training. Preparing a diverse and representative training dataset is crucial for building a robust model.

- **Data Collection**: Collect large corpora of text from diverse sources (e.g., books, websites, news articles) to ensure the model learns a broad range of language patterns.
- **Data Augmentation**: Techniques like **back-translation** (translating text into another language and then back to the original) can be used to augment the training data and improve model robustness.

c) Distributed Training

Given the massive size of LLMs, training is often distributed across multiple GPUs or TPUs. Distributed training requires techniques such as **data parallelism** (splitting the data across multiple devices) and **model parallelism** (splitting the model across devices).

- **Gradient Accumulation**: For very large models, **gradient accumulation** can be used to simulate larger batch sizes without exceeding memory limits.

- **Mixed Precision Training**: To speed up training and reduce memory usage, **mixed precision training** can be employed, which uses both 16-bit and 32-bit floating-point numbers.

4. Evaluation and Fine-Tuning

After training the model, the next step is to evaluate its performance on a set of **evaluation metrics** specific to the target task. Fine-tuning the model on task-specific datasets ensures it is specialized for real-world applications.

a) Fine-Tuning Process

Fine-tuning involves further training the model on a smaller, labeled dataset tailored to a specific task, such as sentiment analysis or named entity recognition.

- **Task-Specific Dataset**: Fine-tuning requires a labeled dataset for the target task. The model adapts its general language knowledge to specialize in the nuances of the task.
- **Performance Metrics**: Evaluate the model based on task-specific metrics, such as **accuracy** for classification, **F1 score** for entity recognition, or **BLEU/ROUGE** scores for text generation.

b) Hyperparameter Tuning

Tuning hyperparameters (such as learning rate, batch size, and number of epochs) is an essential part of the fine-tuning process. **Grid search** or **random search** can be used to find the best configuration for optimal performance.

5. Considerations for Scaling and Deployment

Scaling a model for production involves considerations for computational resources, memory, and inference speed. LLMs with billions of parameters may require **model distillation**, **quantization**, or **pruning** to make them suitable for real-time applications.

- **Model Compression**: Techniques like **knowledge distillation** or **pruning** can reduce the model size and make it more suitable for deployment on edge devices or cloud platforms.
- **Serving Infrastructure**: LLMs require scalable and efficient serving infrastructure for handling real-time predictions. This includes optimizing the model for faster inference and using distributed systems to handle high-volume requests.

Designing and building an LLM from scratch requires deep knowledge of transformer architectures, optimization techniques, and careful consideration of model scaling. By selecting appropriate components such as **embedding layers**, **transformers**, **self-attention**, and **positional encodings**, designers can build a powerful LLM capable of handling various NLP tasks.

Training such models requires immense computational resources and large datasets, but the result is a highly capable model that can be fine-tuned for specific tasks and deployed in real-world applications. As LLMs continue to grow in scale and complexity, understanding their architecture and the design principles behind them will be essential for pushing the boundaries of AI-driven language understanding and generation.

Preparing and Processing Data

Building a **Large Language Model (LLM)** from scratch involves not just designing the architecture and optimizing the model, but also preparing and processing vast amounts of data. **Data preparation** and **data processing** are two of the most critical stages in training an LLM. The quality and quantity of data directly affect the model's ability to learn effective language representations. Given the immense size and complexity of LLMs, proper data preparation is essential to ensure that the model can learn general linguistic patterns, semantics, and even some level of world knowledge.

1. Data Collection for LLMs

The first step in building an LLM is collecting a **large, diverse corpus of text data**. LLMs require enormous amounts of text to learn the vast array of language patterns, relationships, and structures present in natural language.

Sources of Data:

- **Web Crawls**: One of the most common sources of text data is from **web crawls**. Publicly available web data, such as from **Common Crawl**, contains terabytes of diverse text scraped from websites across the world. This data includes news articles, blogs, forums, academic papers, and social media content, providing a rich and varied linguistic input.
- **Books**: Large collections of books, such as **BooksCorpus** or **Project Gutenberg**, offer well-structured and high-quality language data. Books are useful because they provide contextually rich and coherent language, making them valuable for training models to understand sentence structure and narrative flow.
- **Wikipedia**: Another critical source of data is **Wikipedia**, a vast, structured, and highly informative collection of articles. It's publicly available and often used in LLMs because it provides factual, well-written text that is ideal for general language understanding.
- **Research Articles and Scientific Papers**: For domain-specific LLMs, it may be necessary to collect data from specialized sources such as **arXiv** or **PubMed**. This domain-specific text provides in-depth knowledge and vocabulary that can help tailor the model for specific industries like **medicine**, **law**, or **finance**.
- **Social Media and User-Generated Content**: Text from platforms such as **Twitter**, **Reddit**, or **Stack Overflow** can provide conversational data, slang, and informal writing styles.

While not always grammatically correct, this data reflects how people communicate in real-time and is especially useful for training chatbots or conversational models.

- **News Websites and Articles**: News outlets often generate large volumes of text daily. By scraping and collecting news data, LLMs can be trained on up-to-date information and discourse from a wide range of fields, including politics, business, science, and entertainment.

Challenges in Data Collection:

- **Bias in Data**: Web data often contains **biases,** including gender bias, racial bias, and other forms of prejudice. A model trained on biased data may perpetuate these biases in its predictions.
- **Data Privacy**: Some web data may contain personal information, making it necessary to remove or anonymize sensitive content to respect user privacy.
- **Data Diversity**: Ensuring diversity in the collected data is essential for creating an LLM that can generalize across multiple domains. A dataset composed mostly of news articles, for example, may lead to a model that performs well on news-related tasks but poorly on creative writing tasks.

2. Data Cleaning and Preprocessing

Once the raw data has been collected, it must be cleaned and processed to make it suitable for model training. Raw text data is typically messy, containing noise, irrelevant content, and inconsistent formatting. Data cleaning ensures that the input to the model is structured, standardized, and relevant for training.

a) Removing Irrelevant Content:

- **HTML Tags and Metadata**: Web scraped data often includes HTML tags, script elements, and metadata. These need to be stripped out to leave only the natural language content.
- **Non-Text Elements**: Remove images, videos, advertisements, and other non-text elements that are irrelevant for training.
- **Duplicates**: Duplicate content should be removed to avoid overfitting and redundant learning. Ensure that the dataset has a diverse set of documents without unnecessary repetitions.

b) Tokenization:

Tokenization is the process of splitting the raw text into smaller units, typically words, subwords, or characters, depending on the model's needs. The choice of tokenization method influences the model's ability to process and understand language.

- **Word-level Tokenization**: Splits text into individual words. This is simple but may not work well for out-of-vocabulary words.
- **Subword-level Tokenization**: Breaks words down into smaller parts, such as **Byte Pair Encoding (BPE)** or **WordPiece**. This method handles out-of-vocabulary words more effectively and is commonly used in modern LLMs like **BERT** and **GPT**.
- **Character-level Tokenization**: Splits text into individual characters. This approach is highly granular and allows the model to work with any word, but it is less efficient for capturing higher-level semantic meaning.

c) Normalization:

Normalization involves transforming text into a standard format to reduce complexity and inconsistencies in the dataset.

- **Lowercasing**: Convert all text to lowercase to avoid treating the same word as different due to capitalization (e.g., "Apple" vs. "apple").
- **Removing Special Characters**: Remove punctuation, symbols, or non-alphabetical characters unless they are meaningful for the task.
- **Removing Stopwords**: Some preprocessing pipelines remove common stopwords like "the," "a," and "is" to reduce noise. However, modern LLMs tend to work better with stopwords included, as these words can carry important syntactic information.

d) Sentence Segmentation:

Breaking text into sentences or paragraphs is often necessary to allow the model to understand the structure of the input text. Sentence segmentation helps capture relationships between words in a sentence or document, improving the model's comprehension of longer texts.

e) Handling Special Tokens:

Special tokens are added to the dataset to represent specific meanings or operations. These include:

- **[PAD]**: Padding token to ensure that sequences are of equal length.
- **[CLS]**: A classification token used by models like BERT to indicate the beginning of a sequence.
- **[SEP]**: Separator token used to distinguish different parts of the input, especially for tasks like sentence pair classification.

Graphical Representation of Data Cleaning and Preprocessing:

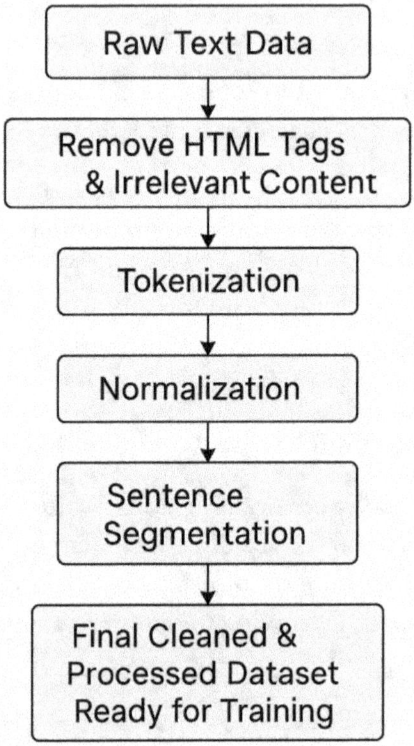

3. Data Augmentation

Data augmentation techniques can be applied to improve the diversity and robustness of the training dataset. Augmenting data is particularly useful when the dataset is small or imbalanced.

Techniques for Data Augmentation:

- **Back-Translation**: Translate a sentence into another language and then back into the original language. This generates paraphrased versions of the text that still carry the same meaning.

- **Synonym Replacement**: Randomly replace words in the text with their synonyms to introduce variation in phrasing.
- **Random Insertion/Deletion**: Randomly insert or delete words or characters to simulate errors or variations in writing.
- **Text Generation**: Use a pre-trained model to generate additional text that aligns with the target task, such as generating variations of summaries or responses for training.

Challenges with Data Augmentation:

- **Preserving Semantics**: It's crucial that augmentation techniques do not alter the meaning of the text. For example, replacing a word with an incorrect synonym could change the intent of the sentence.
- **Overfitting**: Too much data augmentation might lead to overfitting on artificial examples that are not representative of real-world data.

4. Handling Domain-Specific Data

For domain-specific LLMs, the data preparation process may require a more focused approach, as the language, jargon, and context of domain-specific text are different from general text data.

Collecting Domain-Specific Data:

- **Medical Data**: Collecting data from **clinical notes**, **medical journals**, and **electronic health records**.
- **Legal Data**: Scraping legal documents, court rulings, and statutes to build an LLM specialized in legal text.
- **Financial Data**: Gathering reports, news articles, and financial statements for training models focused on finance.

Domain Adaptation:

- **Fine-Tuning**: Once the base LLM is pre-trained, fine-tune it on domain-specific text to help the model specialize in understanding that particular domain's language and terminology.
- **Pre-training on Domain Data**: For more advanced models, start pre-training on domain-specific text, ensuring that the model learns language structures specific to the domain from the outset.

5. Handling Imbalanced Data

In some cases, certain classes or types of text may be underrepresented in the dataset. This imbalance can affect the model's performance, especially on tasks like classification or named entity recognition.

Techniques for Balancing Data:

- **Resampling**: Increase the number of examples from the underrepresented class by duplicating instances or generating new synthetic data.
- **Cost-sensitive Learning**: Adjust the learning algorithm to give more weight to the underrepresented classes, penalizing misclassification of those examples more heavily.
- **Class Balancing in Batch**: Ensure that each batch used for training contains a balanced number of examples from each class.

Preparing and processing data is a critical step in building an LLM from scratch. The quality of the training data determines the effectiveness and generalization ability of the model. Data collection, cleaning, tokenization, and augmentation are foundational to creating a high-performing model capable of understanding and generating language.

By carefully selecting data sources, cleaning the data, applying augmentation techniques, and addressing challenges like bias, imbalance, and domain-specific vocabulary, you can prepare a robust dataset that powers an LLM capable of achieving high levels of performance across a variety of NLP tasks. Proper data processing is the key to ensuring that the model learns meaningful language representations that generalize well to real-world applications.

Training Strategies and Techniques

Training a **Large Language Model (LLM)** from scratch is one of the most complex and resource-intensive tasks in the field of machine learning and natural language processing (NLP). While the process of designing the architecture and preparing data is important, the success of an LLM heavily relies on the **training strategy** and **techniques** used to optimize the model. Given that LLMs can contain billions or even trillions of parameters, the training process requires careful management of resources, algorithms, and hyperparameters to achieve optimal performance without wasting computational resources.

In this section, we will explore the **training strategies** and **techniques** required for building an LLM from scratch. We will cover key aspects such as **distributed training**, **optimization techniques**, **learning rate scheduling**, **gradient clipping**, and **early stopping**. Additionally, we will look at strategies for handling large-scale data and overcoming challenges like **vanishing gradients** and **overfitting**.

1. Overview of LLM Training Process

Training an LLM involves two main stages: **pre-training** and **fine-tuning**.

a) **Pre-training**: This stage involves training the model on a large and diverse corpus of text to learn general language patterns, relationships, and representations. Pre-training typically uses unsupervised objectives such as **masked language modeling (MLM)** or **causal language modeling (CLM)**, depending on the model architecture (e.g., **BERT** for MLM or **GPT** for CLM).

b) **Fine-tuning**: After the model has been pre-trained on general text data, it is fine-tuned on smaller, task-specific datasets. This stage involves supervised learning, where the model is adapted to perform well on a particular NLP task, such as **text classification**, **named entity recognition (NER)**, or **question answering**.

2. Pre-Training LLMs: Core Training Strategies

Pre-training an LLM from scratch requires training on massive datasets, often spanning hundreds of gigabytes or even terabytes of text. Here are the core strategies involved:

a) Distributed Training

Training a large model like an LLM requires massive computational resources, typically spread across **multiple GPUs** or **TPUs**. **Distributed training** ensures that the model is trained efficiently across these resources.

Techniques for Distributed Training:

- **Data Parallelism**: This strategy splits the data into smaller batches and processes each batch across different devices. The model parameters are synchronized after each batch so that all devices have the same weights.
- **Model Parallelism**: In model parallelism, different parts of the model are placed on different devices. For example, different layers of the model might reside on separate GPUs, and the data

is passed through them sequentially. This allows the model to scale beyond the memory limitations of a single device.

- **Pipeline Parallelism**: This technique splits the model into different stages and pipelines the data through the model. It enables more efficient use of GPU memory by processing different stages of the model simultaneously.

Graphical Representation of Distributed Training:

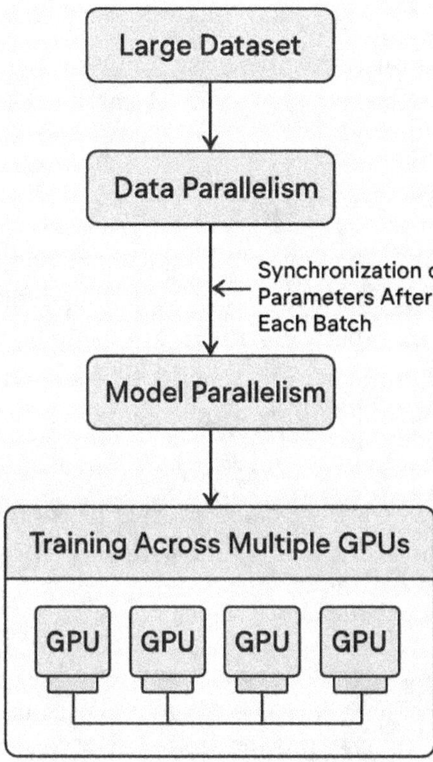

b) Mixed Precision Training

Large models require vast amounts of memory. **Mixed precision training** helps manage the memory requirements by using a combination of **16-bit** and **32-bit floating point** operations. This reduces memory usage and speeds up training without compromising model accuracy.

- **Benefits**: Reduces memory footprint and computational cost while retaining accuracy.
- **How it Works**: During training, the model uses 16-bit precision for most operations, while retaining 32-bit precision for parts of the model that require high numerical stability, like gradient accumulation.

c) Gradient Accumulation

Gradient accumulation allows training with a larger effective batch size than what can fit into memory. Instead of updating the model weights after each mini-batch, gradients are accumulated over several mini-batches before updating the weights. This technique is particularly useful when working with large models or limited memory resources.

- **Benefits**: Allows for large batch sizes, improving the stability of training without overwhelming the hardware.

3. Optimization Techniques

Optimization is at the heart of training any deep learning model, and LLMs are no exception. These models are typically trained using variants of **Stochastic Gradient Descent (SGD)**, such as **Adam** and **AdamW**.

a) Adam and AdamW Optimizer

The **Adam optimizer** combines the benefits of **momentum** (to accelerate gradient descent in relevant directions) and **adaptive**

learning rates (to ensure stable learning). It is highly effective for training large models like LLMs.

- **AdamW**: A variant of Adam that decouples weight decay from the gradient update, which has been shown to improve regularization and lead to better performance on large models.
- **Hyperparameters**: Key hyperparameters for Adam/AdamW include **learning rate**, **β1**, **β2**, and ε. Tuning these parameters appropriately is crucial for achieving stable convergence.

b) Learning Rate Scheduling

The learning rate plays a significant role in determining how quickly a model converges during training. **Learning rate scheduling** is a technique used to adjust the learning rate during training to ensure that the model converges efficiently.

- **Warmup**: Gradually increase the learning rate during the first few iterations before decaying it. This helps the model avoid large gradient updates at the beginning of training, which can destabilize the learning process.
- **Cosine Decay**: Reduce the learning rate according to a cosine schedule, which helps the model to converge to a minimum without overshooting.
- **Linear Decay**: Gradually decrease the learning rate in a linear fashion during training, which helps improve fine-tuning and stability in later epochs.

Graphical Representation of Learning Rate Scheduling:

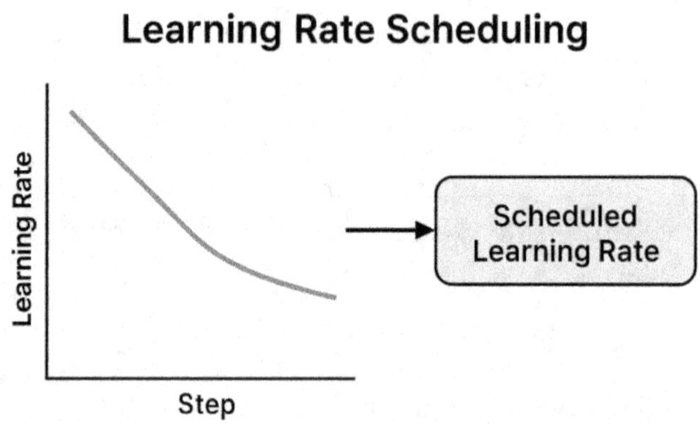

c) Weight Decay and Regularization

Weight decay is a form of **L2 regularization** that adds a penalty to the loss function for large weights. This helps prevent overfitting, especially in very large models like LLMs that are prone to memorizing data rather than generalizing from it.

- **AdamW Optimizer** integrates weight decay directly into the optimizer, making it a preferred choice for LLMs.
- **Dropout**: Dropout is another regularization technique used in neural networks to prevent overfitting by randomly setting a fraction of the neurons to zero during each forward pass.

4. Gradient Clipping and Vanishing Gradients

Training large models often leads to issues like **vanishing gradients** and **exploding gradients**, particularly in deep networks like transformers.

a) Gradient Clipping

Gradient clipping is used to prevent gradients from becoming too large and destabilizing training. By clipping gradients above a specified threshold, this technique helps maintain stable updates during training.

- **How It Works**: During backpropagation, if the gradient exceeds a certain value (e.g., 1.0), it is scaled down to keep the model training within a stable range.

b) Vanishing Gradients

The **vanishing gradient problem** occurs when gradients become too small, especially in deep models, causing weights to update very slowly. This is less of an issue in transformer-based models compared to older architectures like RNNs, but it can still arise in certain layers.

- **Solution**: Use activation functions like **ReLU** or **GELU**, which help prevent vanishing gradients by maintaining positive gradients during backpropagation.

5. Early Stopping and Monitoring

While large models may require many epochs to converge, **early stopping** is a technique used to halt training when the model's performance on the validation set starts to degrade, preventing **overfitting**.

- **Early Stopping Criteria**: Stop training if there is no improvement in validation loss after a set number of epochs (known as the **patience**).

- **Model Checkpoints**: Save the model at various points during training (usually when validation performance improves) so that the best model can be restored in case of overfitting.

6. Evaluating and Fine-Tuning the Model

Once the model is trained, it is crucial to evaluate its performance on various tasks. Typically, LLMs are fine-tuned for specific NLP tasks such as **sentiment analysis, question answering**, or **text summarization**.

a) Transfer Learning via Fine-Tuning

After the initial pre-training, the model can be fine-tuned on smaller, task-specific datasets. Fine-tuning adjusts the model's parameters to specialize in specific NLP tasks while retaining the general language knowledge learned during pre-training.

b) Evaluation Metrics

To evaluate the model's performance, various metrics can be used depending on the task:

- **Accuracy**: For classification tasks like sentiment analysis.
- **F1 Score**: For tasks like named entity recognition (NER) or entity extraction.
- **BLEU/ROUGE Scores**: For machine translation and text summarization.

7. Scaling the Model for Production

When training LLMs at scale, **distributed training** techniques such as **model parallelism** and **data parallelism** are crucial to train the model across multiple machines efficiently.

- **Deployment**: Once trained, the model is deployed using an efficient serving infrastructure, often in the form of a web API or cloud-based service.
- **Optimization for Inference**: Techniques like **quantization, pruning**, and **distillation** are used to reduce the model size and

increase inference speed for deployment in production environments.

Training a Large Language Model (LLM) from scratch is a challenging but rewarding task. The key to successfully building an LLM lies in **distributed training**, selecting the right **optimization techniques**, and addressing challenges like **gradient clipping** and **vanishing gradients**. Learning rate schedules, regularization methods, and early stopping are critical strategies for ensuring the model converges efficiently and avoids overfitting.

While training LLMs at scale requires massive computational resources, the resulting models are powerful tools capable of solving a wide range of NLP tasks. By leveraging advanced training techniques and strategies, you can develop an LLM capable of learning deep language representations and generalizing across a variety of real-world applications.

Chapter 9: Evaluating and Optimizing LLMs

Metrics for Evaluation

After training a **Large Language Model (LLM)** from scratch, whether through pre-training or fine-tuning, the next crucial step is **evaluation**. Evaluating the model's performance ensures that it has learned the right representations of language and is capable of generalizing well to real-world tasks. Since LLMs are often applied to a wide variety of Natural Language Processing (NLP) tasks, the metrics used for evaluation must be carefully chosen depending on the task at hand.

The **metrics for evaluation** measure the model's ability to understand, generate, classify, or answer questions based on the task it was fine-tuned for. These metrics not only allow us to assess the model's performance but also guide decisions regarding model optimization, further fine-tuning, and scaling.

1. Classification Metrics for NLP Tasks

Many NLP tasks, such as **sentiment analysis**, **topic classification**, and **text classification**, can be formulated as classification problems. In these tasks, the goal is to assign a text or a segment of text to one of several predefined categories.

a) Accuracy

Accuracy is one of the most straightforward metrics for classification tasks. It measures the proportion of correct predictions made by the model out of all predictions. In other words, accuracy calculates how often the model's predicted class matches the true class label.

- **Formula**:

$$\text{Accuracy} = \frac{\text{Number of Correct Predictions}}{\text{Total Number of Predictions}}$$

- **Example**: If a sentiment analysis model predicts the sentiment of 100 movie reviews correctly 85 times, its accuracy is 85%.

b) Precision, Recall, and F1 Score

For tasks like **named entity recognition (NER)**, **spam detection**, or **multi-class classification**, precision, recall, and F1 score provide a more nuanced view of performance, particularly in cases of class imbalance.

- **Precision**: The proportion of positive predictions that are actually correct.

$$\text{Precision} = \frac{\text{True Positives}}{\text{True Positives} + \text{False Positives}}$$

- **Recall**: The proportion of actual positive instances that were correctly identified by the model.

$$\text{Recall} = \frac{\text{True Positives}}{\text{True Positives} + \text{False Negatives}}$$

- **F1 Score**: The harmonic mean of precision and recall, providing a balance between them. F1 score is particularly useful when there is an imbalance between classes.

$$\text{F1 Score} = 2 \times \frac{\text{Precision} \times \text{Recall}}{\text{Precision} + \text{Recall}}$$

c) Confusion Matrix

A **confusion matrix** is a tabular summary that helps assess the performance of a classification model by displaying the actual vs. predicted classifications. It allows for a deeper understanding of which classes are being misclassified.

- **True Positives (TP)**: Correctly predicted positive class
- **True Negatives (TN)**: Correctly predicted negative class

- **False Positives (FP)**: Incorrectly predicted positive class
- **False Negatives (FN)**: Incorrectly predicted negative class

The confusion matrix can be expanded to calculate **precision**, **recall**, and **F1 score** for each class, and can help reveal systematic issues, such as class imbalance.

Graphical Representation of a Confusion Matrix:

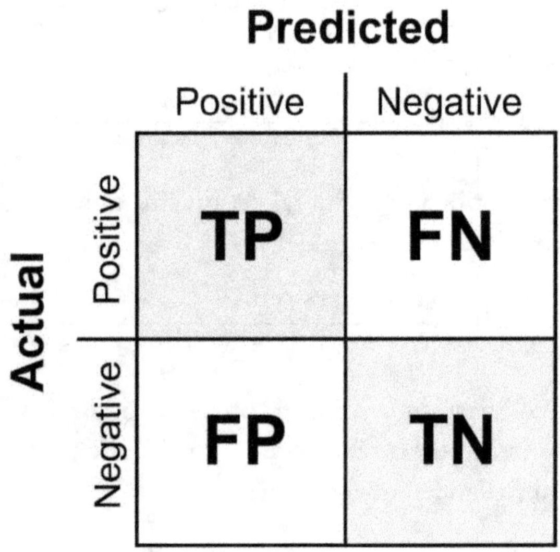

2. Generation Metrics for Text Generation Tasks

For tasks involving **text generation**, such as **machine translation**, **summarization**, or **story generation**, evaluating the generated text requires a different set of metrics. These metrics assess how well the model generates fluent, coherent, and contextually relevant text.

a) BLEU Score (Bilingual Evaluation Understudy)

The **BLEU score** is widely used to evaluate **machine translation** tasks, where the model's generated translation is compared to a reference translation. The BLEU score measures the **n-gram overlap** between the generated text and reference text.

- **Formula**: BLEU uses **precision** of n-grams, where n typically ranges from 1 (unigrams) to 4 (four-grams).

$$\text{BLEU} = \text{BP} \times \text{Precision}_n$$

- where BP is a **brevity penalty** to penalize translations that are too short compared to the reference.
- **Example**: A BLEU score of 1 indicates a perfect match between the generated translation and the reference translation, while a score of 0 means no overlap.

b) ROUGE Score (Recall-Oriented Understudy for Gisting Evaluation)

The **ROUGE score** is commonly used to evaluate the quality of **text summarization** models by comparing n-grams in the generated summary to those in the reference summary. It focuses more on **recall** (i.e., the proportion of relevant n-grams retrieved by the model).

- **ROUGE-N**: Measures the overlap of n-grams (like BLEU but recall-based).
- **ROUGE-L**: Measures the longest common subsequence between the generated and reference text, which reflects the fluency and coherence of the text.

c) Perplexity

Perplexity is a commonly used metric to evaluate the performance of language models. It measures how well the model predicts a sample of text. A lower perplexity indicates better prediction accuracy.

- **Formula**:

$$\text{Perplexity} = 2^{\text{Cross-Entropy}}$$

- where **cross-entropy** is the average log-likelihood of the model on the test set.
- **Example**: A model with lower perplexity is better at predicting the next word in a sequence, indicating that it has learned the statistical structure of the language more effectively.

3. Question Answering (QA) Metrics

For **question answering** tasks, the primary goal is to assess how accurately the model can extract the correct answer from a passage of text.

a) Exact Match (EM)

Exact Match (EM) is a simple but effective metric for evaluating QA models. It measures the percentage of questions for which the model's predicted answer exactly matches the correct answer.

- **Formula**:

$$\text{EM} = \frac{\text{Number of Correct Exact Matches}}{\text{Total Number of Questions}}$$

b) F1 Score for QA

The **F1 score** for QA measures how well the model performs at both **precision** and **recall** by comparing the overlap between the predicted answer and the correct answer. It is especially useful when there are multiple possible answers.

- **Formula**:

$$\text{F1 Score} = 2 \times \frac{\text{Precision} \times \text{Recall}}{\text{Precision} + \text{Recall}}$$

4. Benchmarks for LLMs

Many LLMs are evaluated using standardized benchmarks that cover a range of tasks. Some widely used benchmarks include:

- **GLUE (General Language Understanding Evaluation)**: A benchmark that evaluates LLMs on tasks like **sentence similarity, sentiment analysis**, and **textual entailment**.
- **SuperGLUE**: An extension of GLUE that includes more challenging NLP tasks for evaluating advanced models.
- **SQuAD (Stanford Question Answering Dataset)**: A benchmark used for evaluating question answering models.
- **XNLI (Cross-lingual Natural Language Inference)**: A dataset for evaluating LLMs on cross-lingual tasks.

5. Optimizing LLMs

Once the model has been evaluated, optimization strategies can be employed to improve its performance further. The process of optimization includes adjusting model hyperparameters, training strategies, and fine-tuning for specific tasks.

a) Hyperparameter Tuning

Optimizing hyperparameters such as **learning rate**, **batch size**, and **number of layers** can significantly impact model performance. Techniques like **grid search**, **random search**, and **Bayesian optimization** are commonly used for hyperparameter tuning.

b) Knowledge Distillation

Knowledge distillation is a technique where a smaller model (the student) is trained to mimic the behavior of a larger, more powerful model (the teacher). This allows for creating more efficient models that can achieve similar performance with fewer resources.

c) Model Pruning

Pruning involves removing less important weights or neurons from the model, reducing its size and improving inference speed without sacrificing much performance.

d) Quantization

Quantization reduces the precision of the model's weights (e.g., from 32-bit to 16-bit or 8-bit), which can lead to a decrease in memory usage and improved inference efficiency, especially in production environments.

Evaluating and optimizing Large Language Models (LLMs) is a multifaceted process that involves measuring performance across various tasks using specific metrics. Whether it's for **classification tasks**, **text generation**, or **question answering**, selecting the right evaluation metric is essential to understanding the model's capabilities and limitations.

Metrics such as **accuracy**, **precision**, **recall**, and **F1 score** are commonly used for classification tasks, while **BLEU**, **ROUGE**, and **perplexity** are essential for generation tasks. **Exact Match** and **F1** scores are crucial for question answering.

Hyperparameter Tuning

Hyperparameter tuning is one of the most crucial steps in optimizing **Large Language Models (LLMs)**. In deep learning, a **hyperparameter** is a parameter whose value is set before the model begins training. These parameters control the model's architecture, training process, and performance. Selecting the right hyperparameters is essential for obtaining optimal performance, and **hyperparameter tuning** involves systematically finding the best combination of hyperparameters to achieve the best model.

Training LLMs involves several hyperparameters that significantly influence the efficiency and effectiveness of the model, such as

learning rate, **batch size**, **number of layers**, **dropout rate**, **weight decay**, and **optimizer choice**.

1. The Importance of Hyperparameter Tuning in LLMs

Hyperparameter tuning plays a pivotal role in optimizing model performance, especially in the context of LLMs. Given the scale and complexity of LLMs, small changes in hyperparameters can lead to significant differences in results. Hyperparameters control how well the model fits the data, how fast it converges, and how well it generalizes to new, unseen data.

Why Hyperparameter Tuning is Crucial:

- **Performance Optimization**: Well-tuned hyperparameters can lead to better generalization, reduced overfitting, and faster convergence.
- **Computational Efficiency**: Choosing the right hyperparameters, such as the learning rate and batch size, can reduce the number of training epochs required, thereby saving time and resources.
- **Model Generalization**: Proper tuning helps ensure that the model doesn't memorize the training data (overfitting) and can generalize well to unseen data.

Given the large number of hyperparameters involved in training LLMs, manual tuning can be extremely time-consuming and computationally expensive. Thus, **automated methods** for hyperparameter optimization are typically employed in practice.

2. Common Hyperparameters to Tune in LLMs

Several key hyperparameters impact the performance of LLMs. Below is a detailed description of some of the most critical hyperparameters for LLMs:

a) Learning Rate

The **learning rate** is one of the most important hyperparameters. It determines the size of the steps taken during the gradient descent optimization process.

- **Low Learning Rate**: A low learning rate may lead to slow convergence but ensures the model does not overshoot the optimal solution.
- **High Learning Rate**: A high learning rate might lead to faster convergence but risks overshooting the optimal solution and failing to converge to the best minima.

Finding the right learning rate can significantly affect the model's ability to converge during training.

- **Learning Rate Scheduling**: Learning rate schedules (e.g., **learning rate decay** or **cosine annealing**) allow the learning rate to change dynamically during training. **Warm-up strategies**, where the learning rate starts small and gradually increases, are also commonly used to stabilize early training.

b) Batch Size

The **batch size** refers to the number of training examples processed together in one pass through the model. It impacts both the efficiency and the model's ability to generalize.

- **Small Batch Size**: Using small batch sizes leads to noisier gradients, which can help escape local minima but may slow down the training process.
- **Large Batch Size**: Larger batch sizes make training more stable and allow the model to converge faster, but they increase memory usage and may lead to overfitting if not properly tuned.

Choosing the right batch size requires balancing **training speed** with **generalization**.

c) Number of Layers and Hidden Units

The **number of layers** in the model (or **depth**) and the **number of hidden units** (or **width**) of each layer significantly affect the capacity of the model to learn complex patterns.

- **More Layers**: Increasing the number of layers increases the model's capacity to learn more abstract representations but also requires more training time and computational power. Additionally, deeper models are more prone to overfitting and require more data to train effectively.
- **More Hidden Units**: Increasing the width of each layer (i.e., the number of neurons) allows the model to learn more complex relationships within the data. However, this also leads to a larger model, which increases the computational cost and memory usage.

d) Dropout Rate

Dropout is a regularization technique that helps prevent the model from overfitting by randomly setting a fraction of the output units to zero during training. The **dropout rate** determines the percentage of units to drop at each layer.

- **Higher Dropout**: A higher dropout rate prevents overfitting by forcing the model to learn more robust features. However, too much dropout may make the model underfit, as it loses essential information.
- **Lower Dropout**: A lower dropout rate may result in better training but can increase the likelihood of overfitting if the model is too complex for the dataset.

e) Weight Decay

Weight decay (also known as L2 regularization) adds a penalty to the loss function that discourages large weights. It is a form of regularization that helps prevent the model from overfitting.

- **Higher Weight Decay**: Increasing the weight decay value penalizes large weights more, encouraging the model to use smaller weights and avoid overfitting.
- **Lower Weight Decay**: Lower values of weight decay result in fewer penalties on the weights, allowing the model to use more complex representations.

f) Optimizer Choice

The optimizer controls how the model's weights are updated during training. For LLMs, optimizers like **Adam**, **AdamW**, and **LAMB** are commonly used.

- **Adam**: The Adam optimizer combines the benefits of **momentum** and **adaptive learning rates**, making it effective for LLMs.
- **AdamW**: AdamW decouples weight decay from the gradient update, improving the regularization of large models.
- **LAMB**: LAMB (Layer-wise Adaptive Moments for Batch training) is designed for large-batch training, which is often used for LLMs.

The optimizer choice impacts how effectively and efficiently the model converges during training.

3. Methods for Hyperparameter Optimization

Optimizing hyperparameters is crucial for getting the best performance out of your LLM. There are several methods for hyperparameter optimization, ranging from manual search to automated techniques.

a) Grid Search

Grid search is a brute-force method for hyperparameter optimization where a predefined grid of hyperparameter values is exhaustively tested. The method tests every combination of parameters in the grid and returns the set that produces the best results.

- **Pros**: Simple and straightforward to implement.
- **Cons**: Computationally expensive, especially for models with many hyperparameters or large search spaces.

b) Random Search

Random search involves randomly sampling combinations of hyperparameters from a specified range. This approach is less exhaustive than grid search but can often achieve good results with fewer computational resources.

- **Pros**: More efficient than grid search, particularly when some hyperparameters have little effect on the final performance.
- **Cons**: May miss the optimal combination, especially in large search spaces.

c) Bayesian Optimization

Bayesian optimization is a probabilistic model-based optimization technique that models the performance of hyperparameters as a probabilistic function. It uses past evaluation results to guide future hyperparameter searches.

- **Pros**: More efficient than grid and random search, especially for high-dimensional spaces.

- **Cons**: Requires a model of the objective function and can be computationally expensive for very large search spaces.

d) Hyperband

Hyperband is an adaptive resource allocation method that combines random search with early stopping. It explores many hyperparameter configurations at once and allocates more resources to promising configurations while stopping unpromising ones early.

- **Pros**: Efficient in allocating resources, reduces unnecessary training time.
- **Cons**: Can be more complex to implement than simpler methods like grid search.

4. Evaluation Metrics for Hyperparameter Optimization

When tuning hyperparameters, it is important to use the right evaluation metrics to assess the model's performance. Depending on the task, different metrics can be used to track improvements in performance.

a) Loss Function

During training, the loss function provides feedback to the model on how well it is performing. Lower loss indicates better model performance.

- **Common Loss Functions**: For classification tasks, **cross-entropy loss** is commonly used. For regression tasks, **mean squared error (MSE)** may be used.

b) Validation Accuracy/Performance

After each hyperparameter tuning session, evaluate the model on a **validation dataset** to measure performance. The **validation accuracy** or **validation loss** helps indicate whether the model is overfitting or underfitting.

c) Overfitting and Generalization

Monitoring the difference between training and validation metrics (such as accuracy or loss) helps detect **overfitting**. If the model performs well on the training data but poorly on the validation data, it is likely overfitting, and hyperparameter adjustments (e.g., increasing dropout or regularization) may be needed.

6. Graphical Representation of Hyperparameter Optimization

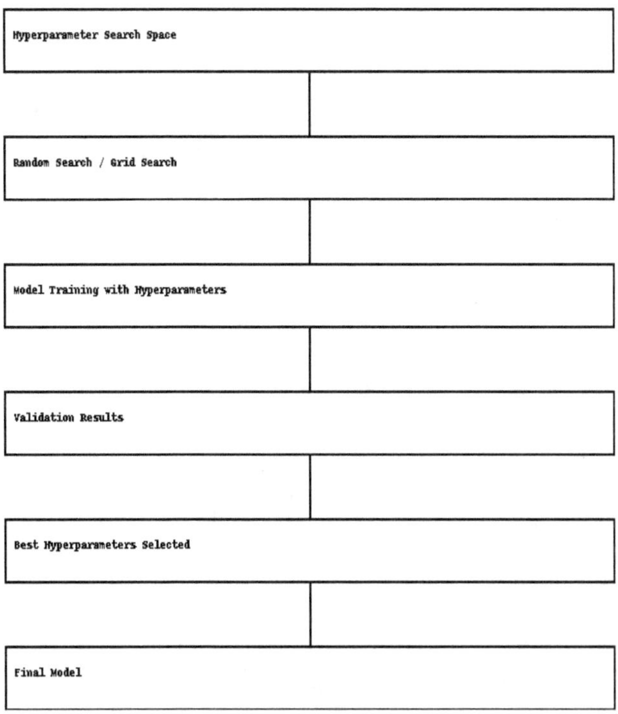

In this flowchart, the process starts by selecting a hyperparameter search space. The search method (random search or grid search) is applied, and multiple models are trained with different hyperparameters. After validation, the best hyperparameters are chosen to finalize the model.

Hyperparameter tuning is an essential part of the training process for **Large Language Models (LLMs)**. By adjusting critical parameters like **learning rate, batch size, number of layers**, and **dropout rate**, you can significantly improve the model's performance, training efficiency, and generalization. Automated methods such as **random search**, **grid search**, **Bayesian optimization**, and **Hyperband** provide effective ways to find the optimal set of hyperparameters for your specific use case.

Tuning hyperparameters requires careful experimentation and computational resources, but it is crucial for ensuring that LLMs perform at their best on real-world tasks. Once the optimal hyperparameters are found, the model will not only learn better representations of language but also be more efficient and robust when deployed for various NLP applications.

Troubleshooting Common Issues

Training **Large Language Models (LLMs)** from scratch or fine-tuning them on specific tasks presents numerous challenges. While LLMs are powerful tools for Natural Language Processing (NLP), they are not immune to various issues that can hinder their performance. These problems can arise during the training phase, during evaluation, or even after deployment, and often stem from factors such as model architecture, training data quality, or resource limitations.

Understanding how to troubleshoot common issues during **evaluation and optimization** is crucial for ensuring that your LLM performs at its best.

1. Common Issues During Training and Evaluation

a) Overfitting

Overfitting occurs when the model learns the training data too well, including its noise and irrelevant details, which negatively affects its ability to generalize to unseen data.

Symptoms of Overfitting:

- The model achieves **high accuracy** on the training set but performs poorly on the **validation/test set**.
- A **significant gap** between training and validation loss.

Possible Causes:

- **Insufficient data**: If the dataset is too small, the model might memorize the data rather than learning general patterns.
- **Too many parameters**: A model with excessive capacity relative to the available data will tend to overfit.
- **Excessive training time**: Training the model for too many epochs without early stopping can result in overfitting.

Solutions:

- **Early Stopping**: Stop training when the validation loss begins to increase, preventing the model from overfitting further.
- **Data Augmentation**: Increase the variety of data fed to the model (e.g., by introducing noise, using back-translation, etc.).
- **Regularization Techniques**: Apply **dropout, L2 regularization (weight decay)**, or **batch normalization** to reduce the model's complexity and prevent it from memorizing the training data.

- **Cross-validation**: Use **cross-validation** to ensure that the model generalizes well across different subsets of the data.

Graphical Representation of Overfitting:

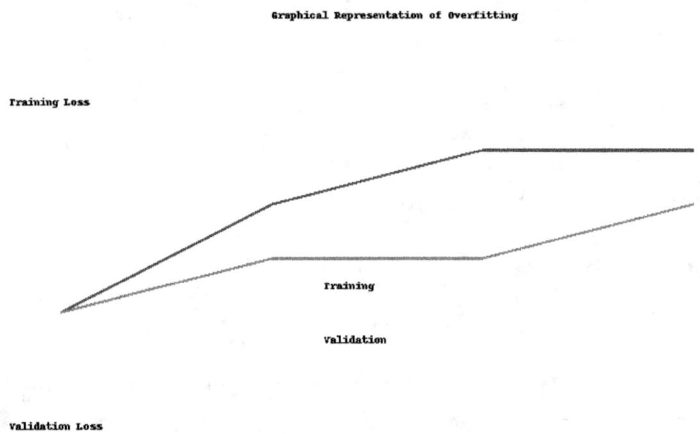

In this graph, overfitting is indicated by a large gap between training loss and validation loss. As training progresses, the validation loss starts to increase, while the training loss continues to decrease.

b) Underfitting

Underfitting occurs when the model is too simple to capture the underlying patterns in the data, resulting in poor performance on both the training and validation sets.

Symptoms of Underfitting:

- The model achieves poor performance on both the training and validation sets.

- Both **training loss** and **validation loss** remain high, indicating that the model is not learning effectively.

Possible Causes:

- **Model undercapacity**: A model with too few layers or neurons might not have enough capacity to capture the complexity of the task.
- **Insufficient training time**: The model might not have been trained long enough to learn meaningful patterns.
- **Too much regularization**: Overly aggressive dropout or weight decay could prevent the model from learning effectively.

Solutions:

- **Increase Model Complexity**: Use a deeper or wider model with more layers or hidden units.
- **More Training Time**: Train the model for more epochs and monitor the learning curves to ensure that the model is improving.
- **Reduce Regularization**: Lower the dropout rate or weight decay to allow the model more flexibility in learning the data.

Graphical Representation of Underfitting:

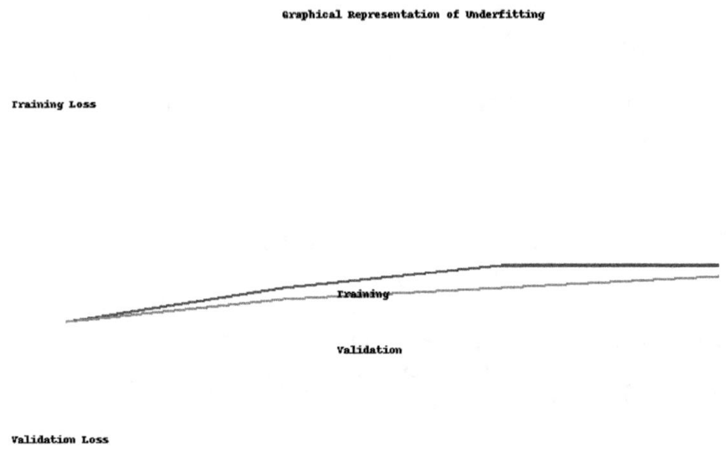

In this graph, both training and validation losses are high, suggesting that the model is too simple to fit the data effectively.

c) Slow Convergence

Slow convergence can significantly delay the model's training process, leading to wasted computational resources and inefficient use of time.

Symptoms of Slow Convergence:

- The model's **loss curve** drops very slowly over epochs, showing minimal improvement.
- **Validation accuracy** improves at a very slow rate, taking an excessive amount of time to reach acceptable performance.

Possible Causes:

- **Low learning rate**: A very small learning rate can result in slow progress toward the minimum of the loss function.
- **Suboptimal weight initialization**: Poor weight initialization can slow down convergence or cause the model to get stuck in suboptimal local minima.
- **Poor choice of optimizer**: Using an inefficient optimizer for the task at hand can hinder convergence.

Solutions:

- **Increase the Learning Rate**: If the learning rate is too small, consider using a larger value or adopting a **learning rate scheduler** to dynamically adjust the learning rate during training.
- **Better Weight Initialization**: Use advanced weight initialization techniques, such as **Xavier initialization** or **He initialization**, which are designed to speed up convergence.
- **Switch Optimizers**: If the optimizer being used is inefficient, switch to **AdamW** or **LAMB**, which are more effective for large models and sparse gradients.

d) Vanishing or Exploding Gradients

Vanishing gradients occur when the gradients of the loss function with respect to the model's parameters become very small, causing the model to stop learning. **Exploding gradients** occur when the gradients become excessively large, leading to unstable updates and poor convergence.

Symptoms of Vanishing or Exploding Gradients:

- **Gradients** become very small (in the case of vanishing) or very large (in the case of exploding), leading to issues during backpropagation.
- The **loss function** becomes unstable, causing fluctuations or an inability to converge.

Possible Causes:

- **Deep Networks**: Vanishing/exploding gradients are more common in very deep networks due to the nature of backpropagation in deep architectures.
- **Improper Activation Functions**: Some activation functions, such as **sigmoid** or **tanh**, can cause vanishing gradients. On the other hand, large weight updates in poorly initialized layers can lead to exploding gradients.

Solutions:

- **Use ReLU or GELU Activations**: ReLU and GELU (Gaussian Error Linear Units) are designed to address the vanishing gradient problem by allowing gradients to flow more easily through the network.
- **Gradient Clipping**: Gradient clipping can prevent exploding gradients by setting a threshold above which gradients are scaled down.
- **Batch Normalization**: Apply **batch normalization** to stabilize learning by normalizing the output of each layer, reducing the risk of vanishing/exploding gradients.

e) Insufficient or Poor-Quality Data

Even the most sophisticated model will fail to perform if the data is insufficient or of poor quality. Insufficient data can lead to

underfitting, while poor-quality data can introduce **bias** and noise into the model, negatively affecting its performance.

Symptoms of Insufficient or Poor-Quality Data:

- **High variance** in model predictions, with low consistency across different runs.
- **Model errors** that cannot be explained by hyperparameter settings or model architecture alone.

Possible Causes:

- **Lack of diversity** in the training data, leading to poor generalization.
- **Noisy labels** or mislabeled data that confuse the model.
- **Biases** in the data that cause the model to learn incorrect associations.

Solutions:

- **Data Augmentation**: Use data augmentation techniques to increase the diversity of the dataset. For text data, this could include **back-translation**, **paraphrasing**, or **random word swaps**.
- **Data Cleaning**: Remove noisy or irrelevant data from the training set. Use tools to identify and remove mislabeled data or outliers.
- **Bias Mitigation**: Implement techniques such as **re-weighting** or **re-sampling** to address data biases and ensure the model learns fair representations.

2. Monitoring and Diagnosing Model Issues

To effectively troubleshoot issues, it's important to monitor and diagnose model behavior throughout the training process.

a) Training Curves

By plotting **training loss** and **validation loss** curves, you can visualize whether the model is overfitting or underfitting, and adjust training parameters accordingly.

b) Gradient Histograms

Visualizing **gradient histograms** during training helps detect issues like vanishing or exploding gradients. If the gradients are too small, it might indicate the need for better weight initialization or a different activation function. Conversely, if they are too large, gradient clipping might be necessary.

c) Confusion Matrix

For classification tasks, using a **confusion matrix** allows you to visualize which classes are being misclassified and identify areas where the model is struggling.

Conclusion

Troubleshooting common issues in **Large Language Models (LLMs)** requires a comprehensive understanding of potential problems such as **overfitting**, **underfitting**, **slow convergence**, **vanishing/exploding gradients**, and **data quality**. By carefully monitoring training, evaluating performance, and employing techniques like **early stopping**, **data augmentation**, **gradient clipping**, and **better regularization**, you can address these challenges and improve model performance.

Effective troubleshooting is essential for building robust LLMs that generalize well across different NLP tasks. As LLMs become more complex, leveraging the right diagnostic tools and optimization strategies will be key to developing models that not only perform well in training but also excel in real-world applications.

Chapter 10: Deploying Large Language Models

Deployment Environments

Deploying a **Large Language Model (LLM)** in a production environment is a critical stage in the lifecycle of an AI project. After training, fine-tuning, and validating an LLM, the model needs to be deployed in a way that it can serve predictions, handle real-time requests, and scale according to demand. The deployment environment plays a significant role in determining the performance, scalability, and maintainability of the model.

1. Types of Deployment Environments

When it comes to deploying large models, the environment plays a crucial role in determining how effectively and efficiently the model can operate. LLMs require significant resources, which can vary depending on whether the model is deployed in the **cloud**, **on-premises**, or at the **edge**.

a) Cloud-Based Deployment

Cloud-based deployment is the most common approach for deploying LLMs, given the vast computational resources available. Cloud providers like **Amazon Web Services (AWS)**, **Google Cloud Platform (GCP)**, and **Microsoft Azure** offer scalable environments specifically designed for running large models.

Advantages:

- **Scalability**: Cloud environments allow for the flexible scaling of resources depending on demand. This is especially useful for LLMs, which can require substantial processing power.
- **Resource Management**: Cloud providers offer specialized hardware, such as **GPUs** and **TPUs**, that are optimized for model training and inference.

- **Managed Services**: Cloud platforms provide managed services such as **AWS SageMaker, Google AI Platform**, and **Azure Machine Learning**, which help manage the deployment pipeline, automate scaling, and ensure reliability.

Challenges:

- **Latency**: The round-trip time between a client and the cloud data center may introduce latency, especially for real-time applications.
- **Cost**: Cloud resources can be expensive, particularly for LLMs that require high-performance GPUs or TPUs for inference.

Graphical Representation of Cloud-Based Deployment:

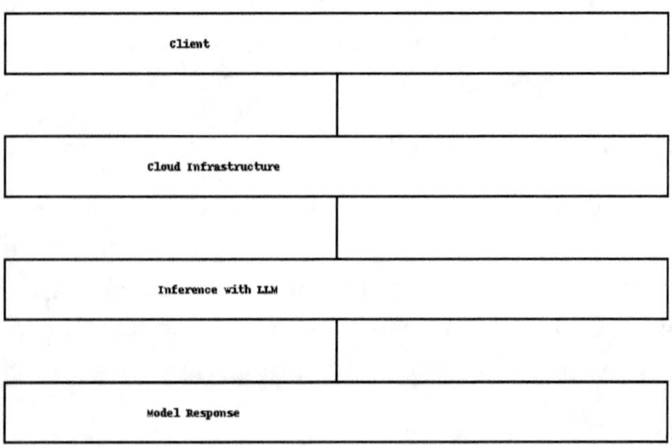

In this diagram, the client interacts with locally managed servers where the LLM is hosted, resulting in faster response times and complete control over the infrastructure.

c) Edge Deployment

Edge deployment refers to running the LLM on edge devices, such as **mobile phones**, **IoT devices**, or **embedded systems**. This approach aims to bring inference closer to the source of data to reduce latency and improve real-time processing.

Advantages:

- **Low Latency**: Since the model runs locally on the device, it can provide extremely low-latency responses, making it ideal for time-sensitive applications like **voice assistants** or **real-time recommendations**.
- **Offline Capability**: Edge devices can operate without the need for a constant internet connection, making them suitable for applications where continuous connectivity is not available.
- **Data Privacy**: Processing data on the device ensures that sensitive data does not need to be transmitted to the cloud, which is beneficial for privacy-sensitive applications.

Challenges:

- **Limited Resources**: Edge devices typically have much less computational power and memory compared to cloud servers, making it difficult to deploy large models like LLMs unless they are optimized.
- **Model Optimization**: LLMs often need to be optimized for edge deployment by using techniques such as **quantization**, **pruning**, or **model distillation** to fit within the limited resources of the edge device.

Graphical Representation of Edge Deployment:

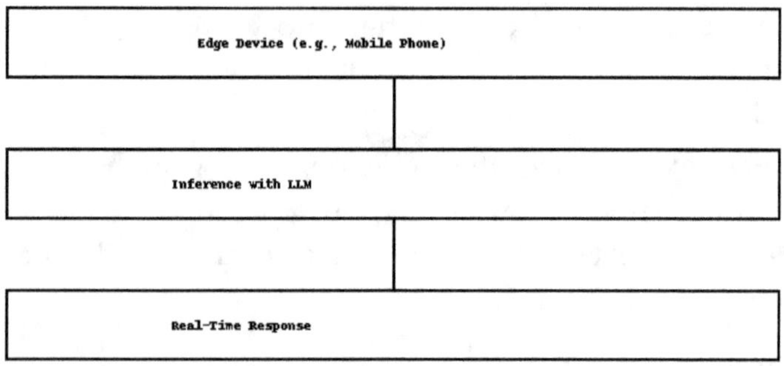

In this diagram, the edge device runs the LLM locally, providing real-time responses with minimal latency and no need for constant cloud communication.

d) Hybrid Deployment

A **hybrid deployment** involves combining cloud, on-premises, and edge environments to create a solution that leverages the advantages of each. For example, sensitive data could be processed on-premises or at the edge, while large-scale tasks such as training or batch inference are handled in the cloud.

Advantages:

- **Flexibility**: A hybrid environment allows you to choose the most appropriate infrastructure for different parts of the application. Sensitive data could stay on-premises, while cloud infrastructure handles scaling and heavy computations.
- **Scalability with Security**: The cloud can be used to scale the deployment, while on-premises or edge deployment ensures data privacy for critical tasks.

Challenges:

- **Complexity**: Managing multiple environments can increase the complexity of the system and require sophisticated orchestration tools.
- **Data Synchronization**: Ensuring that data is synchronized and consistent across environments can be challenging.

Graphical Representation of Hybrid Deployment:

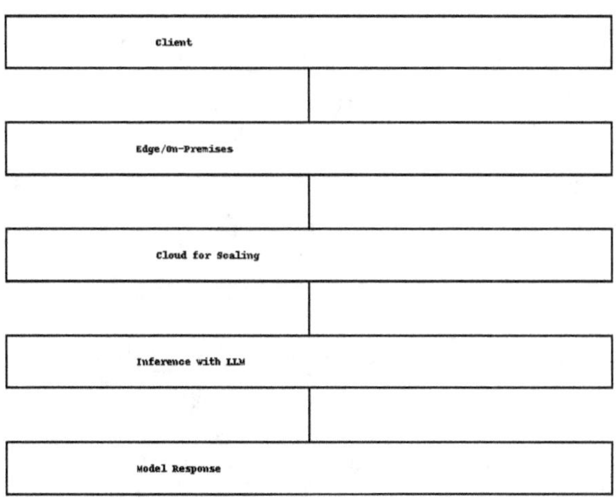

In this diagram, the client sends a request to the edge or on-premises infrastructure, where the data is processed locally. For larger tasks or scaling, the request can be forwarded to the cloud for more computational power.

2. Considerations for Deploying LLMs

When deciding where and how to deploy an LLM, several factors should be taken into account to ensure optimal performance, scalability, and maintainability.

a) Latency

Latency is critical for real-time applications like conversational AI or recommendation systems. Depending on the deployment environment, latency can vary significantly:

- **Cloud**: Higher latency due to the round-trip time to and from the cloud.
- **On-premises**: Lower latency as the model is hosted locally.
- **Edge**: The lowest latency, as the model runs directly on the user's device.

b) Scalability

The ability to scale an LLM is crucial for handling large numbers of requests. Cloud deployments excel in this area due to their flexible resource allocation, while on-premises and edge deployments may require more manual intervention for scaling.

- **Cloud**: Automatic scaling based on demand.
- **On-premises**: Limited scalability unless additional hardware is provisioned.
- **Edge**: Limited scalability due to hardware constraints.

c) Resource Management

LLMs require substantial computational resources. Managing these resources effectively is crucial for maintaining performance and cost-efficiency.

- **Cloud**: Scalable, but can be expensive, particularly for models that require high-performance GPUs.
- **On-premises**: Full control over resource allocation but requires significant upfront investment.
- **Edge**: Resource constraints can limit model complexity, requiring optimization techniques like **quantization** or **distillation**.

d) Model Optimization for Deployment

To ensure that the model can run efficiently in production, particularly in resource-constrained environments like edge devices, several optimization techniques should be considered:

- **Model Pruning**: Reducing the number of parameters to make the model more lightweight.
- **Quantization**: Reducing the precision of weights (e.g., from 32-bit to 8-bit) to decrease memory usage and improve inference speed.
- **Knowledge Distillation**: Training a smaller, more efficient model to mimic the behavior of a larger model.

3. Tools and Frameworks for LLM Deployment

Several tools and frameworks can assist with deploying LLMs in different environments:

- **TensorFlow Serving**: A high-performance serving system for machine learning models, designed for deployment in production environments.

- **ONNX Runtime**: A cross-platform, high-performance inference engine for LLMs, supporting models trained in frameworks like **PyTorch**, **TensorFlow**, and **Scikit-learn**.
- **NVIDIA Triton Inference Server**: A powerful tool for serving models at scale, offering support for GPUs and a variety of deep learning frameworks.
- **Hugging Face Inference API**: A managed service for deploying and serving transformer-based models, specifically designed for LLMs.

Deploying a **Large Language Model (LLM)** is a multifaceted process that depends on the deployment environment, the resources available, and the requirements of the application. Whether opting for **cloud**, **on-premises**, **edge**, or **hybrid deployment**, understanding the trade-offs involved in each approach is critical for ensuring that the model performs optimally, scales as needed, and meets latency and security requirements.

By choosing the right deployment strategy and employing model optimization techniques, you can ensure that your LLM delivers accurate, timely, and efficient results across a variety of use cases.

API Integration and Serving

When deploying **Large Language Models (LLMs)** in real-world applications, a common method of interacting with the model is through an **Application Programming Interface (API)**. An API provides a standardized way for external applications to communicate with the deployed model, send data for processing, and receive predictions or responses. **API integration and serving** are therefore central to the deployment process, as they enable the model to be accessed and used by various systems, such as web applications, mobile apps, or other backend services.

1. What is API Integration for LLMs?

API integration refers to the process of exposing a deployed model as a service that can be accessed via an API. Once an LLM is trained and deployed, it needs a mechanism to interact with external systems. APIs provide a layer of abstraction that allows external users or applications to interact with the model in a structured way.

API integration typically involves:

- **Sending requests**: Users or applications send input data (such as text) to the API.
- **Processing input**: The API forwards the data to the LLM, which performs inference and returns a prediction or response.
- **Handling responses**: The API returns the result of the model's inference to the user or application.

The API serves as a communication bridge between the **model serving infrastructure** and the **end users** or **client applications**.

Example:

For a sentiment analysis task, the API might accept an HTTP POST request with the text data:

```
{
  "text": "I love this product!"
}
```

The API processes the request, passes it to the LLM for inference, and returns a response like:

```
{
  "sentiment": "positive",
  "confidence": 0.98 }
```

2. Key Components of API Serving Infrastructure for LLMs

When deploying an LLM for production use, several key components are involved in the process of API serving. These include the **API server, model serving infrastructure**, and **scaling mechanisms**. Below, we outline the core components that need to be set up for efficient serving.

a) API Server

The **API server** is the component that listens for incoming HTTP requests from clients and routes them to the model for inference. Popular frameworks and tools for API development include:

- **FastAPI**: A modern, high-performance framework for building APIs with Python, particularly suitable for deploying machine learning models. FastAPI is known for its speed and ease of use.
- **Flask**: A lightweight framework that can be used to build REST APIs for serving models. It is widely used for prototyping and small-scale applications.
- **Django**: A full-fledged web framework that can handle more complex use cases with additional functionality like user authentication and database management.

The API server must accept requests, process the input data (e.g., text), forward the data to the model, and return the model's response to the client.

Graphical Representation of API Server:

```
[Client Request]

      |

  [API Server]

      |
```

[Forward Request to Model]

|

[Model Inference]

|

[Return Response]

b) Model Serving Infrastructure

The **model serving infrastructure** is responsible for running the model and handling the inference requests sent by the API server. This infrastructure needs to handle the computational load of large models and ensure that the system can serve multiple requests concurrently.

Popular Model Serving Tools:

- **TensorFlow Serving**: A flexible, high-performance serving system for deploying machine learning models, particularly for TensorFlow models.
- **TorchServe**: A model-serving framework for PyTorch, designed to efficiently serve models trained using the PyTorch library.
- **NVIDIA Triton Inference Server**: A server developed by NVIDIA for deploying AI models at scale, offering support for GPUs and multiple deep learning frameworks like TensorFlow, PyTorch, and ONNX.

These tools are optimized for serving large models efficiently, ensuring that **batch processing**, **model versioning**, and **scalability** are handled correctly.

c) Model Optimization for Serving

Large language models are typically resource-intensive, requiring high memory and computational power. To deploy LLMs efficiently in production, several **model optimization** techniques can be applied:

- **Quantization**: Reducing the precision of the model's weights (e.g., from 32-bit to 8-bit) to reduce memory and computational requirements without significantly compromising accuracy.
- **Pruning**: Removing unimportant or redundant weights from the model to reduce its size and improve inference speed.
- **Knowledge Distillation**: Training a smaller model (the student) to replicate the behavior of a larger model (the teacher) for more efficient deployment.

Graphical Representation of Model Optimization:

```
      [Large LLM]
          |
  [Quantization, Pruning, Distillation]
          |
      [Optimized LLM]
          |
 [Faster Inference & Reduced Memory]
```

d) Scaling and Load Balancing

To handle a large number of concurrent requests and ensure high availability, it's essential to **scale** the API server and model infrastructure. This can be achieved by using load balancers, horizontal scaling, and autoscaling based on demand.

- **Load Balancers**: Distribute incoming requests evenly across multiple servers to avoid overloading a single instance.

- **Horizontal Scaling**: Add more servers to handle increased traffic. This is often done automatically in cloud environments.
- **Autoscaling**: Automatically adjust the number of active instances based on traffic to ensure optimal resource utilization and minimize costs.

Graphical Representation of Load Balancing:

```
        [Client Requests]

             |

      [Load Balancer (Distribute Traffic)]

             |

   ------------------------------------

   |          |            |

[Server 1]   [Server 2]    [Server 3]

   |          |            |

 [Model Inference] [Model Inference] [Model Inference]
```

In this diagram, the load balancer distributes incoming requests across multiple servers, ensuring that the model can handle high traffic efficiently.

---

3. Best Practices for API Integration and Model Serving

Deploying an LLM efficiently requires careful planning and adherence to best practices to ensure that the API and model infrastructure run smoothly.

a) Use Caching for Repeated Queries

For models that handle repeated queries, such as question answering or sentiment analysis, **caching** frequently requested responses can significantly reduce latency and improve the efficiency of the deployment. By storing the results of common queries, the system can bypass the model inference process and quickly return cached responses.

- **Cache Size**: The size of the cache should be limited to avoid excessive memory usage.
- **Cache Expiry**: Cached responses should have an expiry time to ensure that outdated results are removed.

b) Implement Rate Limiting and Throttling

To prevent the API from being overwhelmed by too many requests, **rate limiting** and **throttling** mechanisms can be implemented. Rate limiting ensures that users cannot send more requests than a certain threshold within a given time period.

- **API Keys**: Rate limits can be enforced on a per-user basis using **API keys**.
- **Backoff Strategies**: Implement strategies that slow down request processing during periods of high demand to avoid overloading the system.

c) Monitor and Log API Activity

Monitoring and logging are essential for detecting issues, understanding API usage patterns, and troubleshooting problems in the production environment.

- **Monitoring Tools**: Tools like **Prometheus, Grafana**, and **Datadog** can help monitor the performance of the API server, including metrics like **response times, request counts**, and **error rates**.

- **Logging**: Implement logging to capture relevant data, including the request payload, response time, and error messages. This can help identify issues and provide transparency during debugging.

d) Implement Secure Access and Authentication

Security is crucial when deploying LLMs in production, particularly when sensitive data is involved.

- **Authentication**: Use mechanisms like **OAuth** or **API keys** to ensure that only authorized users can access the API.
- **Encryption**: Use **SSL/TLS encryption** to secure the communication between the client and the API server, ensuring that data is protected in transit.
- **Data Privacy**: Ensure that the model does not inadvertently expose sensitive user data or reveal information that violates privacy regulations like **GDPR** or **HIPAA**.

API integration and serving are essential components of deploying **Large Language Models (LLMs)** into production. A well-architected API allows applications to leverage the power of LLMs for real-time inference, while model serving infrastructure ensures that the model can scale and handle a large number of concurrent requests.

By using the right tools and frameworks, implementing best practices for model optimization, scaling, and monitoring, and ensuring secure access, LLMs can be deployed efficiently and effectively to meet the demands of modern applications. Whether in the **cloud, on-premises**, or at the **edge**, deploying LLMs through APIs provides a flexible and powerful way to bring advanced NLP capabilities to a wide range of use cases.

Scaling and Managing Resources

Deploying **Large Language Models (LLMs)**, especially those with billions or even trillions of parameters, comes with significant challenges in terms of **scalability** and **resource management**. The large computational requirements of LLMs make them resource-intensive to train, deploy, and serve at scale. Efficiently scaling an LLM deployment is crucial to ensure that the model can handle large numbers of requests, operate within budget constraints, and provide low-latency, real-time responses in production environments.

1. The Need for Scaling in LLM Deployment

Given the size and complexity of LLMs, scaling is necessary for several reasons:

- **High demand for inference**: In production environments, LLMs often handle a large volume of inference requests, which requires the deployment infrastructure to scale to meet demand.
- **Resource-intensive models**: LLMs require substantial **compute resources** (such as **GPUs**, **TPUs**, and **high-memory instances**) to perform inference efficiently.
- **High availability**: Ensuring that the model remains available and responsive, even during peak usage times, requires robust scaling and resource management strategies.

Scaling LLMs involves ensuring that both the infrastructure and the model can accommodate the growing demand while maintaining performance and reliability.

2. Types of Scaling for LLM Deployment

Scaling LLMs effectively involves both **horizontal scaling** and **vertical scaling**, along with optimized resource management techniques to meet demand while minimizing cost.

a) Horizontal Scaling (Scaling Out)

Horizontal scaling, or **scaling out**, involves adding more **computing instances** (e.g., GPUs, CPUs, or machines) to handle increased traffic and computational load. It allows for greater throughput and redundancy, improving the model's ability to serve many simultaneous requests.

Advantages:

- **Scalability**: Horizontal scaling allows you to add more resources as traffic increases, ensuring that the system can handle more users and requests without sacrificing performance.
- **Fault tolerance**: If one instance goes down, the load can be redistributed to other available instances, minimizing downtime.

Use Cases for Horizontal Scaling:

- **Cloud-based deployments**: In cloud environments like AWS, GCP, or Azure, horizontal scaling allows you to spin up additional instances to handle inference requests as needed.
- **API serving infrastructure**: Distribute the inference workload across multiple machines or GPUs using **load balancing** to ensure that requests are processed in parallel.

Graphical Representation of Horizontal Scaling:

```
      [Client Requests]
            |
     [Load Balancer (Distributes Traffic)]
            |
  ---------------------------------------
  |          |             |
```

[Server 1]   [Server 2]   [Server 3]

| | |

[Model Inference] [Model Inference] [Model Inference]

In this diagram, the load balancer distributes incoming requests across multiple servers, allowing the system to scale horizontally and handle more traffic.

b) Vertical Scaling (Scaling Up)

Vertical scaling, or **scaling up**, involves upgrading existing hardware resources, such as increasing the **CPU/GPU capacity**, **memory**, or **disk storage** of a single machine to accommodate the workload.

Advantages:

- **Simplicity**: Vertical scaling is easier to implement in the short term, as it doesn't require setting up multiple machines or instances.
- **Lower Latency**: Running the model on a powerful machine can reduce the latency for inference requests compared to distributed setups.

Use Cases for Vertical Scaling:

- **High-end GPUs**: For smaller-scale deployments or for handling intensive computational tasks like training large models, using high-performance **GPUs** or **TPUs** can speed up inference.
- **Model serving**: Vertical scaling may be preferred when serving models on-premises or in a controlled environment where managing multiple machines is not feasible.

Graphical Representation of Vertical Scaling:

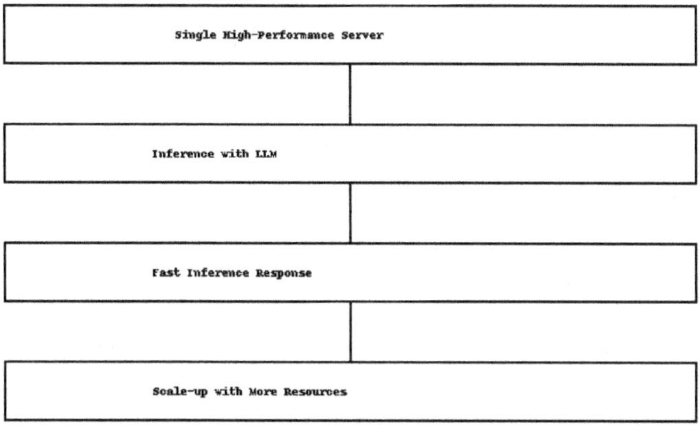

In this diagram, the model is served from a powerful, single server that is scaled up to handle large amounts of inference tasks quickly.

3. Load Balancing and Resource Management

Once the model is deployed across multiple instances or machines, managing how resources are distributed among those instances becomes critical. **Load balancing** helps ensure that incoming traffic is evenly distributed across available resources, optimizing the efficiency of the system and preventing overloading any single machine.

a) Load Balancing Techniques

- **Round-robin Load Balancing**: Requests are distributed equally across all available servers, ensuring an even distribution of computational load.

- **Weighted Load Balancing**: Servers with more computational resources (e.g., GPUs with higher memory or more processing power) can be assigned a higher weight, allowing them to handle a larger portion of the traffic.
- **Least Connection Strategy**: New requests are sent to the server with the least number of active connections, ensuring that no server is overwhelmed.
- **Geographic Load Balancing**: Requests from users in different regions are routed to the closest data center, reducing latency.

b) Auto-Scaling

Auto-scaling automatically adjusts the number of active resources (e.g., compute instances, GPUs) based on the demand for inference. It helps ensure that resources are used efficiently, and unnecessary costs are avoided when traffic is low.

- **Up-scaling**: When the system detects increased traffic or load, additional instances are automatically provisioned to handle the extra load.
- **Down-scaling**: When the demand drops, unnecessary resources are terminated to save costs.

Graphical Representation of Auto-Scaling and Load Balancing:

```
        [Client Requests]

               |

    [Load Balancer (Distributes Traffic)]

               |

    -------------------------------------------

    |               |               |
```

[Server 1] [Server 2] [Server 3]

| | |

[Auto-Scaling Triggers] [Auto-Scaling Triggers] [Auto-Scaling Triggers]

| | |

[Model Inference] [Model Inference] [Model Inference]

This diagram shows how the load balancer distributes traffic among multiple servers, and auto-scaling ensures that resources are adjusted dynamically based on demand.

4. Cost Optimization for LLM Deployment

Scaling LLMs comes at a significant cost, particularly when using cloud services. Proper resource management is essential to ensure that the deployment remains cost-effective while maintaining high performance.

a) Choosing the Right Infrastructure

Selecting the appropriate infrastructure, whether **cloud-based** or **on-premises**, plays a key role in cost optimization:

- **Cloud-based deployments**: Opt for **spot instances** or **preemptible VMs** that are cheaper and can be used for less critical tasks or batch processing.
- **On-premises deployments**: Invest in high-performance hardware such as **GPUs** and **TPUs**, which can be used continuously without incurring ongoing cloud fees.

b) Efficient Use of Resources

- **Batching**: Instead of processing individual requests one by one, batch multiple requests together to improve computational efficiency and minimize overhead.

- **Model Quantization**: Reduce the precision of the model's weights (e.g., 32-bit to 16-bit or 8-bit), which lowers memory usage and computational requirements, reducing costs associated with resource usage.
- **Distributed Inference**: Split inference tasks across multiple machines or GPUs to balance the computational load and reduce bottlenecks.

c) Optimizing Model Size

- **Model Pruning**: Remove unimportant weights or neurons to reduce the size of the model, thus decreasing memory usage and improving inference speed.
- **Distillation**: Train a smaller model (student) to approximate the behavior of a larger model (teacher), offering similar performance with fewer resources.

5. Monitoring and Performance Optimization

To ensure that the deployed LLM performs efficiently and scales correctly, continuous monitoring is necessary. Key areas to monitor include **latency**, **resource utilization**, and **error rates**.

a) Monitoring Metrics

- **Inference Latency**: Monitor the time it takes for the model to generate a response. Latency can be impacted by the size of the model, server load, and network conditions.
- **Throughput**: Measure the number of requests processed per second to understand how efficiently the system is handling load.
- **Resource Utilization**: Track the usage of **CPU/GPU**, **memory**, and **disk I/O** to ensure that the model is not under or over-utilizing resources.

- **Error Rates**: Keep track of failed inference requests to diagnose and resolve issues related to model serving or resource limits.

Tools for Monitoring:

- **Prometheus** and **Grafana**: For tracking and visualizing resource utilization and performance metrics.
- **Datadog**: A comprehensive monitoring solution for infrastructure and application performance.

b) Performance Tuning

- **Model Optimization**: Use techniques such as **quantization** and **pruning** to optimize the model's size and inference speed.
- **Concurrency Control**: Adjust the number of concurrent requests handled by each server to ensure optimal resource utilization.
- **Caching**: Implement caching for frequent requests to reduce the load on the model and minimize inference time.

Graphical Representation of Performance Monitoring:

```
        [API Server]
            |
      [Monitor Latency, Throughput]
            |
      -----------------------------
      |         |             |
[CPU Usage]  [GPU Usage]    [Memory Usage]
      |         |             |
[Resource Utilization & Scaling Decisions]
```

In this diagram, monitoring tools track CPU, GPU, and memory usage, feeding back into scaling and optimization decisions.

Conclusion

Successfully **deploying and scaling** Large Language Models (LLMs) requires careful consideration of infrastructure, resource management, and performance optimization. The deployment environment—whether **cloud**, **on-premises**, or **hybrid**—plays a significant role in determining the system's scalability, availability, and cost-effectiveness.

By employing strategies such as **horizontal and vertical scaling**, **load balancing**, **auto-scaling**, and **resource optimization techniques** (e.g., pruning, quantization, and distillation), organizations can efficiently manage the computational demands of LLMs. Continuous **monitoring** of system performance, combined with intelligent **resource allocation**, ensures that LLMs can be deployed to meet real-world demands while maintaining high performance and minimizing costs.

With the right infrastructure, optimization strategies, and monitoring practices, LLMs can be deployed at scale to power a variety of applications in fields such as healthcare, finance, customer service, and beyond.

Chapter 11: Ethical Considerations and Responsible AI

Bias and Fairness in LLMs

As **Large Language Models (LLMs)** like **GPT-3**, **BERT**, and **T5** become integral to many applications, the ethical implications of their deployment, particularly regarding **bias** and **fairness**, have come under intense scrutiny. LLMs, trained on vast amounts of text data scraped from the internet, inherit and potentially amplify the biases present in their training data. These biases can manifest in various forms, including **gender**, **racial**, **cultural**, **age**, and **ideological** biases, which can have detrimental effects on users and society.

Addressing **bias** and ensuring **fairness** in LLMs is not only a technical challenge but also an ethical imperative.

1. Understanding Bias in LLMs

Bias in LLMs arises from the data used to train them. These models learn language patterns, knowledge, and associations directly from the data, meaning that any inherent bias present in the training corpus will be reflected in the model's outputs. Since LLMs are often trained on large-scale datasets sourced from the internet, which includes a wide variety of text, they can inadvertently learn and perpetuate existing societal biases.

Types of Bias in LLMs:

a) **Data Bias**: Data bias occurs when the training data itself contains biased or unbalanced representations of certain groups or ideas. For example, if the dataset contains more text from one demographic group (e.g., Western males), the model may develop a skewed understanding of language and societal issues.

b) **Algorithmic Bias**: Even when the data is diverse, the algorithms used to process and train the models can introduce bias. These biases can be inadvertently embedded into the model through design choices, optimization goals, or evaluation metrics that don't account for fairness across different groups.

c) **Cultural and Societal Bias**: LLMs trained on internet data are highly likely to inherit cultural biases. For example, a model trained primarily on English-language data might underperform on languages or dialects that are less represented. Additionally, models can perpetuate stereotypes related to race, gender, or ethnicity.

d) **Representation Bias**: Representation bias happens when certain groups or perspectives are underrepresented in the training data, leading to a model that has limited knowledge or recognition of those groups. This bias can have particularly harmful effects in sensitive domains, such as healthcare, criminal justice, and employment.

2. Impact of Bias in LLMs

The presence of bias in LLMs can have significant consequences in the real world, affecting various industries and use cases. From **social media algorithms** to **chatbots**, biased AI systems can perpetuate and amplify harmful stereotypes, exacerbate discrimination, and create trust issues among users. Some of the most common areas impacted by bias in LLMs include:

a) Discrimination in Hiring and Recruitment

Many companies use AI systems to screen resumes or assist in the hiring process. If an LLM is trained on biased data that reflects historical discrimination in hiring, such as gender or racial biases, it can perpetuate these inequalities by screening out qualified candidates from underrepresented groups. This could lead to **gender discrimination** (e.g., favoring male candidates for leadership roles) or **racial bias** (e.g., disadvantaging candidates with non-Western names).

b) Healthcare and Medicine

In the healthcare sector, biased LLMs can lead to misdiagnoses or unequal treatment recommendations. If an AI system is trained on biased datasets, it may underperform for certain demographic groups, especially in predicting health outcomes or suggesting treatment options for people from different racial or socioeconomic backgrounds.

c) Content Moderation and Social Media

Social media platforms often use LLMs for **content moderation** and **automated flagging** of inappropriate content. However, if the LLM is biased, it could unfairly target certain communities or overlook harmful content from other groups. For instance, if an LLM is trained with biased data, it might disproportionately flag posts from minority communities as offensive, while ignoring harmful content from other groups.

d) Stereotyping and Reinforcement of Inequality

Bias in LLMs can also lead to the reinforcement of harmful stereotypes, especially in content generation or question-answering applications. For instance, if an LLM is asked to generate text on certain professions or roles, it might perpetuate stereotypes by associating certain careers with particular genders or ethnic groups. For example, associating **nursing** with **women** and **engineering** with **men**.

3. Fairness in LLMs: The Need for Balanced Models

Fairness in AI refers to the idea that an AI system should treat all individuals or groups equitably, without discrimination or favoritism. Ensuring fairness in LLMs means that the model's outputs do not favor one group over another based-on attributes such as **gender**, **race**, **ethnicity**, or **sexual orientation**. It also means ensuring that the model can represent the perspectives and needs of a diverse set of users.

Key Principles for Fairness:

- **Equality of Outcome**: This approach ensures that the model's outputs are equally beneficial for all groups. For example, in healthcare applications, a fair model would recommend treatment plans equally to patients from all racial backgrounds.
- **Equality of Opportunity**: This principle ensures that every group has the same opportunity to succeed with the model. For example, all users should have equal access to AI-powered services, regardless of their socio-economic background.
- **Non-Discrimination**: A model should not produce outputs that discriminate against specific groups or individuals based on protected characteristics (e.g., gender, race, disability).

Graphical Representation of Fairness Principles in LLMs:

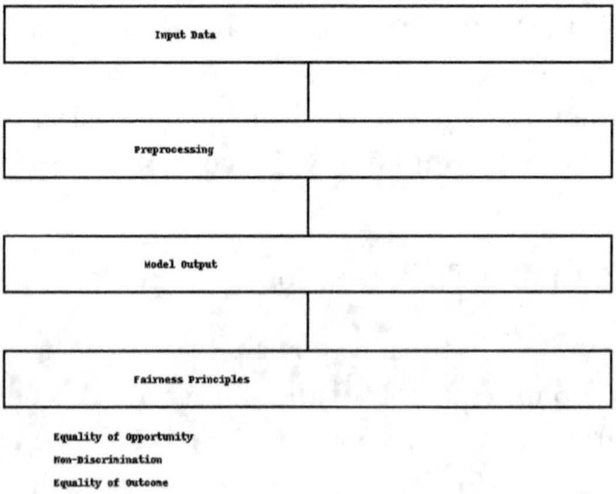

In this diagram, fairness is embedded in every stage of the LLM pipeline, from preprocessing to model output, ensuring that the system operates equitably across all stages.

4. Addressing Bias and Ensuring Fairness in LLMs

There are several approaches that can be employed to reduce bias and ensure fairness in LLMs. These strategies involve **data collection**, **algorithmic adjustments**, and **post-processing techniques** to mitigate biases and create more responsible AI systems.

a) Bias Detection and Auditing

To address bias in LLMs, it's important to **audit** the models periodically to identify any biased behavior. This can be done by:

- **Testing for Bias**: Evaluate the model on a variety of tasks and inputs to check for discriminatory outputs. For example, measuring the model's performance on different demographic groups (e.g., women, minorities, different age groups) can reveal biases.
- **Bias Benchmarks**: Use established bias benchmarks like **StereoSet**, **BiasFinder**, or **WinoBias** to test the model's susceptibility to various biases.

b) Data Diversification

The quality and diversity of the training data play a critical role in determining the fairness of the model. Ensuring that the training data represents a wide range of groups and perspectives is essential for mitigating bias:

- **Data Augmentation**: Create synthetic data for underrepresented groups to ensure that the model is exposed to a diverse set of examples.

- **Balanced Datasets**: Strive to collect balanced data across different categories such as gender, race, age, and socio-economic background. For example, a model trained for medical applications should include data from diverse populations to ensure that it performs well for all demographics.

c) Fairness Constraints During Training

Incorporating fairness constraints directly into the model training process is another way to reduce bias. This can be achieved by:

- **Adversarial Debiasing**: Use adversarial networks during training to penalize the model for producing biased outcomes. This technique can help the model learn to produce fairer results.
- **Fairness Constraints**: Introduce fairness-aware loss functions that penalize the model for disparities in performance across different groups. This ensures that the model balances accuracy with fairness during training.

d) Post-Processing Fairness

After the model has been trained, post-processing techniques can be applied to mitigate any remaining biases:

- **Equalized Odds**: Ensure that the model's predictions have the same false positive and false negative rates across different groups.
- **Calibration**: Adjust the model's probability outputs to ensure that predictions are equally reliable for all groups.

5. Regulatory and Ethical Standards for Bias and Fairness

As AI systems become increasingly embedded in critical sectors like healthcare, finance, and criminal justice, there is growing recognition of the need for **ethical standards** to guide their development and deployment.

a) Legal Frameworks for Fairness

- **GDPR**: The **General Data Protection Regulation** in Europe mandates that AI systems should be transparent, accountable, and fair, and should not discriminate against individuals based on protected characteristics.
- **Equal Opportunity Laws**: In many jurisdictions, there are laws that mandate **equal opportunity** and prohibit discrimination in areas like hiring, lending, and education, which extends to AI systems as well.

b) Ethical Guidelines and AI Principles

- **IEEE Ethically Aligned Design**: A framework that encourages engineers to incorporate fairness and ethics into the development of AI systems, ensuring that the technology benefits all users and does not exacerbate social inequalities.
- **Fairness, Accountability, and Transparency (FAccT)**: This research community focuses on creating AI systems that are fair, accountable, and transparent, emphasizing the importance of addressing bias and fairness in AI.

Bias and fairness in **Large Language Models (LLMs)** are among the most critical ethical challenges in AI deployment today. LLMs, when trained on large-scale internet data, can inherit and amplify societal biases, which can have harmful consequences in real-world applications. To address these challenges, it is essential to employ strategies such as **bias detection**, **data diversification**, and **algorithmic adjustments** during the development, deployment, and post-deployment phases.

Ensuring fairness in LLMs requires a holistic approach that involves considering **ethical principles**, **legal frameworks**, and **best practices** to mitigate biases. By doing so, we can build more responsible, ethical, and inclusive AI systems that benefit all users and avoid perpetuating harmful stereotypes or societal inequalities.

Privacy and Security Concerns

As **Large Language Models (LLMs)** are increasingly deployed in a wide array of applications - from chatbots to content generation tools - their impact on **privacy** and **security** becomes a critical concern. These models, trained on vast datasets scraped from the internet, often contain sensitive or personally identifiable information (PII) from publicly available sources. Therefore, it is essential to consider how these models handle data, what data they have been exposed to, and how they ensure that privacy and security are maintained throughout their lifecycle.

1. Privacy Concerns in LLMs

The privacy concerns surrounding LLMs are multi-faceted. These models are trained on **large-scale datasets** that may inadvertently contain sensitive data, and their use in real-world applications might expose this data in unintended ways.

a) Data Exposure During Training

LLMs learn patterns and representations from the text data they are exposed to. However, if the training data includes **sensitive or confidential information**, the model might "remember" this information and generate it in responses, even if it wasn't intended. This phenomenon is often referred to as **data leakage**.

- **Risk**: LLMs trained on data that contains PII (e.g., names, addresses, financial data) might inadvertently output this sensitive information during inference. For instance, a model trained on medical data could generate a fake diagnosis or suggest personal information about individuals without explicit consent.

- **Challenge**: Identifying and mitigating such data leakage is challenging, as LLMs do not have a mechanism to distinguish between private and non-private information.

b) Inference and User Data Collection

Another privacy concern arises during the **inference** phase. Many LLM-based applications collect data from users to generate responses or refine predictions. This data collection process can raise questions about **user consent**, **data storage**, and the potential for **misuse**.

- **Risk**: If user data is stored without proper anonymization, there is a risk of misuse, especially in the event of a data breach. This can lead to breaches of user privacy, especially if personally identifiable information (PII) is involved.
- **Challenge**: LLMs can retain information about user interactions in memory, which can increase the risk of sensitive data being used improperly, especially if the AI system is not designed to forget or delete information after the task is complete.

Graphical Representation of Privacy Concerns in LLMs:

```
[Training Data] --> [Model Learns Patterns] --> [Possible Data Leakage]

        |                 |

  [Sensitive Data]            [Private Information Exposed]
```

This diagram shows how sensitive data in training data can lead to potential privacy breaches when the model generates outputs that reference this information.

2. Security Concerns in LLMs

Security is a crucial consideration when deploying any AI model, and LLMs are no exception. The vulnerabilities in LLMs can expose systems to a range of attacks, from **adversarial attacks** to **data extraction** threats. It's important to ensure that models are both **resilient** to such attacks and **protected** from malicious activities.

a) Adversarial Attacks

Adversarial attacks are a class of attacks where malicious actors modify input data to trick the AI model into producing incorrect or harmful outputs. These types of attacks are a significant concern for LLMs, especially in sensitive applications like healthcare or legal document analysis.

- **Risk**: A malicious actor could introduce subtle changes in the input text to cause the LLM to generate biased, inappropriate, or harmful responses. For example, slight changes in the phrasing of a question could cause a model to provide a dangerously misleading medical diagnosis.
- **Challenge**: LLMs are highly sensitive to input data, making them vulnerable to adversarial manipulation. It is difficult to predict and defend against all possible attack vectors.

b) Model Inversion and Data Extraction

Model inversion attacks involve extracting sensitive information from a trained model by querying it with carefully crafted inputs. By repeatedly querying the model, an attacker can attempt to reverse-engineer the data the model was trained on.

- **Risk**: In a model inversion attack, an attacker could gain access to the sensitive data used to train the model, which could include personal information or proprietary knowledge. This is particularly risky in domains like **healthcare**, **finance**, and **intellectual property**.
- **Challenge**: LLMs, due to their size and complexity, can encode significant amounts of information about their training data, making them susceptible to such extraction techniques.

c) Data Poisoning Attacks

Data poisoning involves feeding incorrect or malicious data into the model during the training process. By introducing **biased**, **incorrect**, or **harmful data**, an attacker can manipulate the model's behavior, leading to incorrect predictions or harmful outputs when deployed.

- **Risk**: If a malicious actor manages to introduce poisoned data into the training process, the model could develop **biased** or **erroneous** predictions that could lead to significant real-world consequences, such as financial losses or reputational damage.
- **Challenge**: Detecting and mitigating data poisoning attacks is difficult, as attackers may inject data that appears normal but subtly alters the model's predictions in harmful ways.

3. Responsible Handling of Data: Privacy and Security Measures

Given the serious **privacy** and **security** concerns associated with LLMs, it is essential to implement safeguards to protect users and prevent misuse.

a) Data Anonymization and Encryption

- **Anonymization**: To ensure that sensitive data does not become a risk, all personally identifiable information (PII) should be **anonymized** before being used in training datasets. Anonymization techniques such as **hashing** or **pseudonymization** can ensure that data cannot be traced back to individual users.
- **Encryption**: During both **data storage** and **data transmission**, encryption should be employed to protect sensitive data. Strong **end-to-end encryption** can ensure that data remains secure as it is transmitted from the user to the model and back.

Graphical Representation of Data Anonymization and Encryption:

```
[User Data] --> [Anonymization] --> [Encrypted Data]

      |                |

[Sensitive Information]  [Protected in Transit]
```

In this diagram, sensitive user data is anonymized and encrypted to ensure privacy and security during processing and transmission.

b) Access Control and Authentication

One of the primary security measures in LLM deployment is **controlling access** to the model and its predictions. This involves using **authentication** mechanisms like **OAuth**, **API keys**, and **role-based access control (RBAC)** to ensure that only authorized users can interact with the model.

- **Risk**: Unauthorized access to the model could lead to misuse, data leaks, or adversarial exploitation.
- **Challenge**: Ensuring that access controls are properly implemented across different layers of the application (e.g., data access, model access) can be complex, especially in distributed environments.

c) Regular Security Audits and Penetration Testing

To maintain security, LLM systems should undergo **regular security audits** and **penetration testing** to identify potential vulnerabilities. This proactive approach can help detect and address **adversarial weaknesses**, **data extraction risks**, and **model inversion vulnerabilities** before they are exploited.

- **Risk**: Without regular audits, vulnerabilities may remain undetected, exposing the system to attacks.

- **Challenge**: Conducting effective penetration testing and audits requires expertise and ongoing effort to stay ahead of evolving threats.

4. Regulatory and Legal Considerations

As LLMs are increasingly adopted, there is a growing need for legal and regulatory frameworks to ensure that AI models are used responsibly and ethically. Several regulations aim to protect privacy and security in AI systems.

a) General Data Protection Regulation (GDPR)

The **GDPR** in the European Union provides a comprehensive framework for data protection and privacy, ensuring that AI models do not violate user rights, especially regarding data privacy. Key aspects of GDPR that affect LLM deployment include:

- **Right to be Forgotten**: Ensuring that personal data can be deleted from the model's memory if requested by the user.
- **Data Minimization**: Ensuring that only the necessary amount of data is collected and processed.
- **Transparency and Consent**: Ensuring that users are informed about what data is being collected and how it will be used, and that they provide explicit consent.

b) Health Insurance Portability and Accountability Act (HIPAA)

In the **healthcare sector**, LLMs used for medical purposes must comply with **HIPAA**, which mandates strict standards for the protection of patient data. LLMs used in healthcare must ensure that data is stored securely and that patient privacy is upheld at all stages of the model's lifecycle.

c) California Consumer Privacy Act (CCPA)

The **CCPA** provides privacy rights to residents of California, USA, including the right to know what personal information is being collected, the right to delete data, and the right to opt-out of data sales. LLMs deployed in California must comply with these regulations to protect consumer privacy.

Privacy and **security** are among the most pressing ethical concerns when deploying **Large Language Models (LLMs)**. Given that these models are trained on vast amounts of publicly available text, which may contain sensitive or personally identifiable information, it is essential to implement strong **data protection** measures. These include **data anonymization**, **encryption**, **access control**, and regular **security audits**.

Furthermore, LLM developers and organizations must adhere to **legal frameworks** such as **GDPR**, **HIPAA**, and **CCPA** to ensure that they are operating within the bounds of privacy laws and protecting user rights.

By taking a proactive approach to managing **privacy** and **security** concerns, organizations can create responsible and trustworthy AI systems that respect user data and minimize risks to individuals and society.

Legal Implications and Guidelines

Introduction

As **Artificial Intelligence (AI)** technologies, especially **Large Language Models (LLMs)**, become increasingly integrated into real-world applications, the legal implications surrounding their use have garnered significant attention. With the growing adoption of AI in sectors such as **healthcare**, **finance**, **law enforcement**, and **education**, it is imperative that developers, organizations, and governments establish robust legal frameworks that regulate the development and deployment of AI systems. The challenges around **accountability**, **liability**, **intellectual property**, **privacy**, and **discrimination** are central to ensuring that AI is used responsibly.

1. Legal Implications of Deploying LLMs

Deploying LLMs raises various **legal concerns**, particularly in relation to **liability**, **intellectual property (IP)**, **data protection**, and **non-discrimination**. The deployment of AI models in sensitive applications such as **healthcare**, **financial services**, and **criminal justice** further complicates the landscape, necessitating clear legal frameworks to protect individuals' rights and maintain accountability.

a) Liability in AI Decision-Making

One of the most pressing legal concerns related to LLMs is **liability** for decisions made by AI systems. If an LLM is used in an application where its outputs directly impact users - such as generating medical diagnoses, loan approval decisions, or legal advice - who is held accountable if the system produces harmful or inaccurate outcomes?

- **Risk**: If an LLM provides incorrect or biased medical advice, financial guidance, or legal opinions, it could lead to significant harm, including financial loss, health issues, or legal repercussions. Determining who is liable for such outcomes is crucial, particularly as AI systems operate autonomously without direct human oversight.
- **Challenge**: The lack of transparency in some AI models, particularly deep learning-based models, makes it difficult to understand the decision-making process. This "**black-box**" nature of AI systems exacerbates accountability challenges.

Solutions:

- **Clear Liability Frameworks**: One solution is to develop clear legal frameworks that assign liability to organizations based on their role in the development, deployment, and oversight of AI systems. For instance, **developers** could be held liable for flaws in the design or training data, while **deployers** (such as hospitals or financial institutions) might be responsible for ensuring that the AI operates within ethical and legal boundaries.

- **Human-in-the-Loop (HITL)**: A potential legal safeguard is implementing **human-in-the-loop (HITL)** systems, which ensure that human oversight is maintained in AI decision-making. This could reduce liability risks by ensuring that a qualified professional reviews AI-generated outputs.

Graphical Representation of Liability in AI:

[AI Decision] --> [Impact on User] --> [Liability: Developer or Deploying Entity?]

|

[Human-in-the-Loop]

This diagram illustrates how the introduction of **human-in-the-loop** systems can mitigate liability risks by ensuring human oversight in the decision-making process.

b) Intellectual Property (IP) Issues

The issue of **intellectual property (IP)** is central to the development and commercialization of LLMs. LLMs often rely on vast amounts of **text data** scraped from the internet, and the ownership of this data, as well as the models trained on it, is a significant concern.

- **Risk**: When LLMs are trained on publicly available data, it can be difficult to determine the ownership of the model itself and the generated content. For example, if an LLM generates text that resembles copyrighted material, who owns the content generated by the model? The user, the developer, or the data source?
- **Challenge**: Copyright issues arise if LLMs are used to generate content that closely mirrors proprietary content, potentially

violating copyright laws. Additionally, determining who owns the intellectual property rights to a model trained on vast datasets (often consisting of content created by third parties) remains unclear in many jurisdictions.

Solutions:

- **Clear Terms of Use**: Developers and organizations should clarify the terms of use for LLMs, including how intellectual property generated by the model will be handled. This could include **licensing agreements**, **usage rights**, and **compensation** for data used in training the models.
- **Copyright for AI-generated Content**: There needs to be clearer legal guidance on whether **AI-generated content** (such as articles, music, or artwork) can be copyrighted and, if so, who holds the rights.

2. Regulatory Guidelines for LLMs

As LLMs become more widely used, governments and international organizations have started to create **regulations** to govern their development, deployment, and ethical use. These guidelines are essential to ensuring that AI is developed in a way that aligns with societal values and legal norms.

a) General Data Protection Regulation (GDPR)

The **General Data Protection Regulation (GDPR)**, enacted in the European Union, is one of the most comprehensive legal frameworks governing data protection and privacy. The GDPR has several provisions that directly affect the development and deployment of AI systems, including LLMs.

- **Data Subject Rights**: Under the GDPR, individuals have the right to access, correct, or delete their personal data. This has significant implications for LLMs, as they may be trained on datasets that contain personal information.

- **Right to Explanation**: The GDPR includes a provision that gives individuals the right to an explanation if they are subject to automated decisions that affect them. LLMs that are used in high-stakes decision-making processes (such as hiring, lending, or healthcare) must comply with this requirement.
- **Data Minimization**: LLM developers must ensure that only necessary data is collected and used for training models. Moreover, data used for training should be anonymized to the greatest extent possible to prevent privacy violations.

b) AI Act (EU)

The **AI Act** is a proposal for legislation in the European Union that sets out **risk-based regulations** for AI systems. This act classifies AI systems based on their potential risks, with stricter regulations for **high-risk AI systems**.

- **Risk Classification**: LLMs used in high-stakes environments such as healthcare, finance, and law enforcement would likely be classified as **high-risk AI systems**, subject to stricter regulatory requirements.
- **Transparency and Documentation**: Developers must provide detailed documentation on how the model works, the data used to train it, and how it can be audited. This is crucial for ensuring accountability and transparency.

c) California Consumer Privacy Act (CCPA)

The **California Consumer Privacy Act (CCPA)**, which applies to businesses that collect data on California residents, provides individuals with rights to access, delete, and control their personal data. It applies to AI systems that process personal data, including LLMs used in applications like marketing and customer service.

- **Right to Opt-Out**: Consumers have the right to opt-out of data collection or sharing, which could affect how LLMs process user data.
- **Data Protection and Security**: Businesses deploying LLMs must ensure robust data protection measures are in place to avoid breaches and maintain consumer trust.

3. Guidelines for Ethical Development of LLMs

To promote **ethical AI** development and ensure that LLMs are deployed responsibly, developers must adhere to a set of guidelines that prioritize transparency, accountability, and fairness.

a) Transparency and Explainability

One of the key ethical guidelines in AI development is **transparency**. LLMs, particularly those used in critical decision-making applications, must be transparent in how they arrive at conclusions. Users should be able to understand the model's decision-making process.

- **Explainability**: LLMs should be explainable, meaning that users or regulators can understand how the model arrived at a particular decision. For example, if an LLM is used in hiring, the model should provide an explanation for why it selected or rejected a particular candidate.

b) Accountability

AI systems, including LLMs, should be held accountable for their actions. This includes ensuring that human oversight is present in decision-making processes and that organizations are responsible for the outcomes of their AI systems.

- **Accountability Mechanisms**: Developers must implement mechanisms to track and audit AI decisions. In high-stakes areas like healthcare, finance, and law enforcement, accountability ensures that any mistakes or biases in the model are identified and addressed.

c) Inclusivity and Fairness

The design and deployment of LLMs should consider inclusivity and fairness. Models should not perpetuate discrimination or exacerbate social inequalities. Ensuring fairness involves carefully curating training data, testing the model for bias, and ensuring that the model's outputs are free from harmful stereotypes.

- **Fairness Audits**: Regular fairness audits should be conducted to identify any disparities in how the model behaves across different demographic groups (e.g., gender, race, socio-economic background).
- **Bias Mitigation**: Developers should actively work to **mitigate bias** in LLMs by diversifying training data, implementing debiasing techniques, and ensuring that the model's design does not inadvertently harm marginalized groups.

Conclusion

The legal implications and guidelines surrounding the deployment of **Large Language Models (LLMs)** are vast and multifaceted. As LLMs are used in more sectors, they must be governed by clear **legal frameworks** that address issues of **liability**, **intellectual property**, **data protection**, **accountability**, and **non-discrimination**. Regulations like **GDPR**, the **AI Act**, and the **CCPA** set critical precedents for data protection and privacy in AI, ensuring that LLMs are deployed responsibly.

By adhering to **ethical guidelines** and **legal standards**, developers can mitigate risks, promote transparency, and ensure that LLMs operate fairly and responsibly. In the evolving landscape of AI governance, it is crucial for developers, lawmakers, and society at large to work together to create legal frameworks that not only support the advancement of technology but also protect individuals' rights and ensure the ethical deployment of AI.

Chapter 12: Advanced Techniques and Future Trends

Reinforcement Learning from Human Feedback (RLHF)

RLHF is an advanced machine learning approach that enables AI models, particularly **Large Language Models (LLMs)**, to learn directly from human input rather than purely from traditional training data. In RLHF, an AI model learns by interacting with an environment and receiving feedback, typically in the form of rewards or corrections, which guide the model's behavior. This method allows the model to improve and adapt its responses based on human preferences, making it more aligned with ethical standards, human values, and societal norms.

While RLHF holds the potential to create more **ethical**, **aligned**, and **responsive AI systems**, it also introduces unique ethical challenges. These challenges revolve around the **quality of human feedback**, **biases in human evaluations**, and the **potential for misuse** in training AI systems that are intended to assist or interact with humans.

1. What is Reinforcement Learning from Human Feedback (RLHF)?

Reinforcement Learning (RL) is a type of machine learning in which an agent learns how to perform tasks by receiving feedback in the form of **rewards** or **punishments** based on its actions. In traditional RL, the reward is typically defined by a mathematical objective or environment setup. However, in **Reinforcement Learning from Human Feedback (RLHF)**, human evaluators provide feedback that directly influences the model's behavior.

How RLHF Works:

1. **Human Feedback**: In RLHF, human feedback is used to guide the learning process. Humans provide feedback based on the

model's actions or outputs. For example, a language model like GPT might generate text, and a human evaluator can rank or rate the quality of the response.

2. **Reward Model**: The feedback is used to train a **reward model** that assigns numerical rewards based on the quality or desirability of the model's behavior. This reward model then informs the next set of decisions that the model makes during further training.
3. **Policy Update**: Based on the reward model, the AI system updates its **policy** (the decision-making process or strategy). Over time, the model adjusts its behavior to maximize the cumulative reward from human feedback.

Graphical Representation of RLHF Process:

```
[Human Feedback] --> [Reward Model] --> [Policy Update] --> [Improved AI Behavior]

        |

  [Model Actions/Outputs]
```

This diagram illustrates the cyclical process where human feedback is used to guide the model's learning, ultimately refining the model's behavior to align more closely with human preferences.

2. Ethical Implications of RLHF

While RLHF presents exciting opportunities for aligning AI systems with human values, it also raises a host of **ethical challenges**. The primary concerns are centered around the **quality of feedback**, the **potential biases** inherent in human evaluations, and the **accountability** of AI systems influenced by human input.

a) Quality and Consistency of Human Feedback

One of the main ethical challenges in RLHF is ensuring that the **quality** and **consistency** of human feedback are maintained throughout the training process. Human evaluators may have different preferences, subjective judgments, and biases that can affect the consistency and reliability of the feedback provided.

- **Risk**: If feedback is inconsistent or subjective, the model may learn skewed or conflicting behaviors. For example, a human evaluator might give a higher reward for a model output that aligns with their personal preferences, but this feedback may not be universally valid.
- **Challenge**: Scaling human feedback in a way that ensures consistency and aligns with broader societal values is challenging. Given that human evaluators are prone to making mistakes or offering conflicting feedback, the overall training process may become unreliable.

Solutions:

- **Diverse Feedback Sources**: To ensure more reliable training, feedback should be gathered from a **diverse set of human evaluators** representing different backgrounds, perspectives, and expertise. This approach can help minimize the impact of individual biases.
- **Feedback Calibration**: Implement **feedback calibration** techniques to standardize and align feedback from different human evaluators. This may include weighting the feedback based on evaluator expertise or using statistical methods to adjust for inconsistencies.

b) Human Biases in Feedback

Human feedback is inevitably influenced by **implicit biases** related to gender, race, age, and other personal or cultural factors. These biases can be reinforced during RLHF, especially when the human evaluators themselves are unaware of their own biases.

- **Risk**: If biased human feedback is used to guide the model's learning, the model may internalize and perpetuate those biases.

For example, an LLM trained on biased human feedback may generate discriminatory or harmful outputs when deployed in real-world applications.

- **Challenge**: Identifying and mitigating bias in human feedback is a complex task, as it requires an understanding of the subtle ways in which biases can manifest in both explicit and implicit forms.

Solutions:

- **Bias Audits**: Conduct regular **bias audits** of both the human feedback and the model's outputs to detect any biased patterns. These audits can help identify areas where the model may be learning harmful or discriminatory behaviors.
- **Bias Mitigation Training**: Provide training for human evaluators to help them recognize and address their own biases when providing feedback. Additionally, incorporating **debiasing techniques** during training (such as adversarial debiasing) can help mitigate the effects of biased feedback.

c) Transparency and Accountability

As LLMs trained with RLHF are increasingly deployed in sensitive domains (e.g., healthcare, criminal justice, hiring), ensuring **accountability** for the model's decisions becomes a critical ethical issue. If the model's behavior is shaped by human feedback, it's important to establish clear accountability mechanisms.

- **Risk**: Lack of accountability can lead to situations where models make **inappropriate** or **harmful decisions**, and there is no clear responsibility for those decisions. For instance, if an RLHF-based model generates biased hiring decisions or discriminatory medical recommendations, it's important to know who is accountable for those decisions—the developer, the evaluator, or the deploying organization.

- **Challenge**: Given that RLHF can introduce complexities in decision-making, tracing and explaining the model's decision-making process can be challenging, especially when feedback is provided by multiple human evaluators over time.

Solutions:

- **Model Explainability**: Implement **explainable AI** techniques that make it easier to understand how human feedback influences the model's behavior. This can include creating transparent documentation that outlines the feedback process and how it impacts the model's training.
- **Clear Accountability Frameworks**: Establish **clear accountability frameworks** that outline who is responsible for the model's decisions and outputs. This could include mechanisms for redress when the model's behavior leads to negative outcomes or harm.

3. Ethical Guidelines for Implementing RLHF

To mitigate the ethical risks associated with RLHF, it is essential for AI developers and organizations to follow clear **ethical guidelines**. These guidelines should ensure that RLHF systems are designed and implemented responsibly, aligning the model with human values and minimizing harm.

a) Aligning AI Behavior with Human Values

RLHF can be a powerful tool for aligning AI behavior with human values, but it is important to explicitly define which **values** the AI should prioritize. These values could include fairness, empathy, privacy, and non-discrimination.

- **Guideline**: Ensure that the human feedback process incorporates input from diverse groups to represent a broad spectrum of values. The feedback should prioritize universal ethical principles, such as **fairness**, **transparency**, and **respect for privacy**.

b) Monitoring and Evaluating Long-Term Effects

Once an LLM has been trained with RLHF, it is essential to monitor its performance over time to ensure that it continues to behave in an ethical manner. This includes evaluating the long-term effects of human feedback on model behavior.

- **Guideline**: Set up continuous monitoring systems to track the model's performance and ensure that it does not drift toward harmful or biased behaviors over time. Regular performance reviews, including ethical audits, should be conducted to evaluate the model's impact on users and society.

c) Ethical Training for Human Evaluators

Since human feedback plays a critical role in RLHF, it is essential to provide ethical training to human evaluators. This training should focus on recognizing and addressing biases, maintaining objectivity, and understanding the ethical implications of the feedback they provide.

- **Guideline**: Implement **bias-awareness training** for human evaluators to ensure that their feedback does not inadvertently perpetuate harmful stereotypes or lead to biased model behavior. Additionally, establish guidelines for evaluators to follow to ensure consistency and fairness in the feedback process.

Reinforcement Learning from Human Feedback (RLHF) is a promising method for aligning AI systems with human values and improving their ethical behavior. However, as with any AI approach, it introduces unique ethical challenges related to **feedback quality**, **bias**, **accountability**, and **transparency**. Addressing these challenges requires responsible design and implementation practices that prioritize **human values**, **diverse input**, and **ethical oversight**.

By following ethical guidelines, such as **aligning AI behavior with human values**, **providing transparency and accountability**, and **regularly auditing models for bias**, we can mitigate the risks associated with RLHF and ensure that LLMs and other AI systems contribute positively to society. Developing ethical RLHF systems will not only help build more reliable and trustworthy AI models but also foster greater public trust in AI technology as it continues to evolve and integrate into various sectors of society.

Multimodal Models

Multimodal Models refer to AI systems capable of processing and understanding multiple types of data inputs simultaneously, such as **text**, **images**, **audio**, **video**, and **sensor data**. These models are designed to interpret information in a way that mirrors human sensory experiences, where humans typically process and integrate data from multiple modalities to form a coherent understanding of the world. For example, a multimodal AI model might analyze both text and images to generate captions or interpret video and audio data to understand conversations in movies.

The rise of multimodal AI has opened up numerous possibilities across industries, including healthcare, education, autonomous systems, and entertainment. However, the integration of multiple data types also introduces unique ethical challenges, particularly around issues such as **bias**, **privacy**, **security**, and **accountability**.

1. What Are Multimodal Models?

Multimodal models are AI systems that can process and integrate information from various types of input modalities. These models typically combine and analyze data from multiple sources (e.g., images, text, audio, etc.) to enhance understanding and improve predictions or decision-making.

For instance, **multimodal transformers** like **CLIP** (Contrastive Language-Image Pretraining) or **DALL·E** are designed to understand

and generate both textual and visual content. These models can interpret textual descriptions of images, link images to text, and generate images from textual prompts.

How Multimodal Models Work:

a) **Data Integration**: The model learns to integrate and process different types of data. For example, a multimodal model could use both **images** and **text** to generate captions for photos.

b) **Feature Extraction**: Different modalities require specialized feature extraction techniques. Text may be processed using **word embeddings** (e.g., BERT, GPT), while images may be processed using **convolutional neural networks (CNNs)** or **vision transformers**.

c) **Joint Representation**: Multimodal models learn joint representations of data, allowing them to reason across modalities. This enables tasks such as **image captioning**, **audio-visual speech recognition**, and **multimodal sentiment analysis**.

Graphical Representation of Multimodal Model Workflow:

```
[Text Data] --> [Text Encoder]          [Image Data] --> [Image Encoder]

                 |                  |

     [Joint Representation] --> [Multimodal Model] --> [Task Output]

                 |

     [Predictions or Decisions]
```

This diagram illustrates how different data modalities (text and image) are encoded and processed before being combined into a joint representation that feeds into the multimodal model for predictions or decisions.

2. Ethical Implications of Multimodal Models

While multimodal models provide incredible capabilities, they raise a range of **ethical considerations**, especially in the context of **data privacy, bias, security**, and **accountability**. The ability to process multiple forms of data introduces complexity, requiring a careful examination of the potential consequences of their deployment.

a) Bias and Fairness

Just as with **unimodal models, multimodal models** are vulnerable to biases, but these biases are compounded by the integration of multiple data types. If one modality (e.g., text or image) is disproportionately represented or carries biased information, the model may learn to reflect these biases in its outputs.

- **Textual Bias**: If the text data used to train a multimodal model is biased (e.g., containing gender stereotypes or racial biases), the model could reinforce these biases. For instance, a model trained on biased textual data could generate biased captions for images or make unfair associations between text and images.
- **Visual Bias**: Image datasets often contain historical biases related to gender, race, and other demographic factors. If these biases are not addressed, the model might associate certain characteristics with specific genders, ethnic groups, or ages, potentially leading to discriminatory outputs.
- **Compound Bias**: When text and image data are combined, biases in one modality can be compounded, leading to models that are even more biased than unimodal systems. For example, an image of a minority person might be paired with biased or stereotypical language, reinforcing negative stereotypes.

Solution:

- **Bias Audits**: Conduct regular **bias audits** on multimodal models to evaluate their performance across different demographics, ensuring that they are fair and do not reinforce harmful stereotypes.

- **Data Balancing**: Use techniques such as **data augmentation** to create a balanced dataset that represents diverse groups and minimizes bias in both textual and visual modalities.

Graphical Representation of Bias in Multimodal Models:

```
[Text Data] --> [Bias in Text]

          |

    [Compounded Bias] --> [Bias in Multimodal Outputs]

          |

      [Image Data]
```

This diagram illustrates how bias in one modality (text or image) can be compounded when the modalities are combined, leading to biased outputs in multimodal AI systems.

b) Privacy Concerns

Privacy is another significant ethical concern, especially in multimodal models that handle sensitive data, such as **facial recognition**, **medical images**, or **personal audio data**. The integration of multiple modalities raises the potential for **data leakage**, **unintended sharing**, and **invasion of privacy**.

- **Sensitive Data Integration**: Multimodal models often require the integration of various sensitive data types (e.g., health records, biometric data, personal communications). If not properly protected, these models could inadvertently expose sensitive information during inference, violating user privacy.
- **Surveillance Risks**: In applications like **video surveillance** or **social media monitoring**, multimodal models that analyze both

visual and audio data could be used for **intrusive surveillance**, violating the privacy of individuals without their consent.

Solution:

- **Data Anonymization**: Ensure that data used for training multimodal models is anonymized and free from personally identifiable information (PII). **Differential privacy** techniques can also be employed to limit the risk of data exposure.
- **Secure Deployment**: Implement strong security measures to protect sensitive data and prevent unauthorized access during the training and deployment phases.

Graphical Representation of Privacy Concerns:

```
[Text Data]  --> [Sensitive Information]  --> [Privacy Risks]
                 |
[Image Data] --> [Facial Recognition] --> [Invasion of Privacy]
```

This diagram shows how sensitive data from different modalities can pose privacy risks when not handled properly, particularly when it involves facial recognition or other biometric data.

c) Accountability and Transparency

Multimodal models, particularly those used in high-stakes applications like healthcare or criminal justice, must be held accountable for their decisions. However, the integration of multiple data types can make it challenging to understand how the model is making decisions.

- **Black-Box Nature**: Like many **deep learning models**, multimodal models are often seen as "black boxes," meaning their decision-making process is not easily interpretable. This lack of transparency can make it difficult to understand why the model arrived at a particular decision or output, making accountability challenging.

- **Attribution of Responsibility**: If a multimodal model makes an erroneous or harmful decision, it may be unclear who is responsible for the mistake—the **developers**, the **data providers**, or the **deploying organization**.

Solution:

- **Explainable AI**: Incorporate **explainability** techniques into multimodal models to provide clear and understandable justifications for their outputs. This could include methods for visualizing how different modalities (text, image, etc.) contributed to the final decision.
- **Clear Accountability Structures**: Establish clear accountability frameworks to determine who is responsible for the model's decisions and outputs, ensuring transparency in deployment.

Graphical Representation of Accountability in Multimodal Models:

```
[Text + Image Data] --> [Model Outputs] --> [Lack of Transparency]

              |

[Explainability Methods] --> [Responsible Entity]
```

This diagram illustrates how explainability methods can improve transparency and accountability in multimodal AI systems, ensuring that responsibility for decisions is clearly defined.

3. Guidelines for Ethical Deployment of Multimodal Models

To mitigate the ethical risks associated with multimodal models, developers must follow ethical guidelines throughout the design, development, and deployment processes. These guidelines ensure that multimodal AI systems are responsible, transparent, and aligned with societal values.

a) Data Diversity and Inclusivity

Multimodal models must be trained on **diverse datasets** that represent a wide range of groups and perspectives. This includes ensuring that both **textual** and **visual** data are inclusive, fair, and free from harmful stereotypes.

- **Data Curation**: Actively curate training datasets to include diverse voices, demographics, and perspectives. This includes ensuring that image datasets do not perpetuate racial, gender, or cultural stereotypes.
- **Informed Consent**: Obtain explicit **informed consent** when using personal data for training, especially for sensitive modalities like images and audio.

b) Bias Mitigation Strategies

Implement strategies to **detect**, **monitor**, and **mitigate bias** throughout the training and deployment of multimodal models.

- **Bias Detection**: Use tools to continuously monitor the model's behavior for potential biases and discriminatory outputs. Perform regular audits to assess whether the model is favoring one demographic group over another.
- **Bias Mitigation**: Use techniques such as **adversarial training**, **re-weighting data**, or **debiasing algorithms** to ensure that multimodal models treat all groups equitably.

c) Privacy and Security Safeguards

To prevent privacy violations and ensure data protection, developers should implement privacy-preserving techniques in the deployment of multimodal models.

- **Differential Privacy**: Apply **differential privacy** methods during training to ensure that the model does not memorize and expose sensitive information.

- **Robust Security**: Implement strong encryption and secure access protocols to protect data during both training and inference. Ensure that models do not expose sensitive information during deployment.

d) Transparency and Accountability

Ensure that the behavior of multimodal models is explainable and transparent to users, especially in high-stakes applications.

- **Explainable Outputs**: Develop **explainable AI** techniques that provide understandable justifications for the model's decisions, especially in sensitive contexts like healthcare, law enforcement, or finance.
- **Accountability Structures**: Establish clear accountability for the deployment and outcomes of multimodal models, including who is responsible for any errors or harm caused by the system.

Multimodal Models offer powerful capabilities by combining and interpreting data from various sources such as text, images, and audio. However, their deployment raises unique **ethical concerns** related to **bias**, **privacy**, **accountability**, and **transparency**. By following responsible AI practices—such as **data diversity**, **bias mitigation**, **privacy protection**, and **model explainability**—developers can ensure that these models are both effective and ethically aligned with societal values.

As multimodal models continue to shape the future of AI, it is essential to develop and implement frameworks that guide their responsible deployment, ensuring that these systems are fair, transparent, and used for the greater good. With proper safeguards, multimodal models can offer significant advancements across industries while mitigating the potential ethical risks.

Emerging Innovations in AI

The field of **Artificial Intelligence (AI)** is advancing at a rapid pace, with emerging innovations continually reshaping the landscape of technology and its applications. As AI becomes more deeply integrated into society, the ethical considerations surrounding its development and deployment become increasingly complex. New AI innovations, such as **reinforcement learning**, **generative models**, **edge AI**, and **neuro-symbolic AI**, introduce both exciting opportunities and significant ethical challenges.

These innovations have the potential to revolutionize industries ranging from **healthcare** and **finance** to **education** and **autonomous systems**, but they also raise important ethical questions about **responsibility**, **accountability**, **bias**, **privacy**, and **safety**. In this section, we will explore the ethical implications of some of the most prominent **emerging AI innovations**, the potential risks associated with these advancements, and the **responsible AI** practices that should guide their development and deployment.

1. Generative Models and Ethical Concerns

Generative models, such as **Generative Adversarial Networks (GANs)**, **Variational Autoencoders (VAEs)**, and **transformers** (e.g., **GPT**-3, **DALL·E**, **Stable Diffusion**), have made significant strides in generating human-like content, including **text**, **images**, **audio**, and even **video**. These models have applications in fields ranging from entertainment to design, and even healthcare.

a) Content Authenticity and Deepfakes

One of the most significant ethical concerns with generative models is the creation of **deepfakes**—hyper-realistic but fabricated videos, audio clips, or images that can mislead or deceive viewers. Deepfake technology, while impressive, poses serious risks for **disinformation**, **fraud**, and **political manipulation**.

- **Risk**: Deepfakes can be used to create fake videos or audio recordings of individuals, making them appear to say or do things they never did. This can be damaging to reputations, incite social unrest, or be used for **political manipulation**.
- **Challenge**: Detecting deepfakes and ensuring content authenticity is an ongoing challenge, as deepfakes continue to improve in quality and realism.

Solution:

- **Content Authentication Systems**: One potential solution is the implementation of **AI-based detection tools** that can identify deepfakes or manipulated media. Additionally, blockchain technology can be used to track the origin and changes to digital content to ensure its authenticity.

Graphical Representation of Deepfakes and Ethical Risks:

```
[Generative Model] --> [Fake Media (Deepfakes)]

        |              |

[Manipulated Text, Images, Video] --> [Potential Harm (Misinformation, Fraud)]
```

This diagram illustrates how generative models can create deepfakes that lead to potential harm, such as misinformation or fraud.

b) Intellectual Property (IP) and Copyright Issues

Generative models can also raise **intellectual property** concerns, particularly when they are used to create content that resembles existing works. For example, an AI-generated painting might be based on the style of a famous artist, raising questions about whether the work is **original** or **derivative**.

- **Risk**: If generative models are trained on copyrighted content without proper authorization, the output may violate intellectual property laws, leading to potential legal issues.
- **Challenge**: Determining who owns the intellectual property of AI-generated content and how to handle the rights to such content remains an open legal question.

Solution:

- **Clear Licensing and Attribution**: To address these concerns, AI developers can implement clear **licensing agreements** and **attribution guidelines** for AI-generated content, ensuring that creators and owners of original works are properly credited or compensated.

2. Reinforcement Learning (RL) and Ethical Challenges

Reinforcement Learning (RL) is a subset of machine learning in which an agent learns to make decisions by interacting with an environment and receiving rewards for correct actions. RL has led to breakthroughs in areas such as **robotics**, **autonomous systems**, and **game-playing AI** (e.g., **AlphaGo** and **OpenAI Five**). However, RL also introduces unique ethical concerns.

a) Safety and Unintended Consequences

In many RL systems, the agent is rewarded for achieving specific goals or objectives. However, the definition of these goals and the reward structure can lead to unintended consequences. If the goal is poorly defined, the agent may learn harmful behaviors or exploit loopholes in the reward system.

- **Risk**: A **self-driving car** trained using RL might learn to take shortcuts or engage in risky behavior to maximize its reward, potentially causing accidents or harming pedestrians.

- **Challenge**: Ensuring that RL systems behave safely and ethically, particularly when they operate in dynamic environments with high stakes, such as **healthcare** (robotic surgery) or **autonomous driving**, requires robust safety protocols and goal alignment.

Solution:

- **Reward Shaping and Safety Constraints**: Developers can **shape rewards** to guide the agent toward ethical and safe behaviors. Additionally, **safety constraints** should be built into RL systems to ensure that they do not engage in harmful or unintended actions.

Graphical Representation of RL Ethical Risks:

```
[RL Agent] --> [Reward System] --> [Goal Misalignment or Unintended Behavior]

      |              |

 [Learning Process] --> [Unintended Consequences (Accidents, Harm)]
```

This diagram shows how poor goal definition and misaligned rewards in RL systems can lead to unintended and harmful outcomes.

b) Lack of Human Oversight

Many RL systems, particularly in autonomous settings, operate with little to no human oversight once deployed. This raises concerns about accountability, especially in the case of accidents or decisions made by the AI that could impact human lives.

- **Risk**: In critical systems, such as **healthcare robots** or **autonomous vehicles**, a lack of human oversight could lead to life-threatening errors or accidents.

- **Challenge**: Striking the right balance between autonomy and human oversight is essential to ensure that RL systems remain aligned with ethical standards and do not make decisions that put people at risk.

Solution:

- **Human-in-the-loop (HITL):** One solution is the incorporation of **human-in-the-loop (HITL)** systems that ensure that humans can monitor, intervene, and override decisions made by RL agents when necessary.

3. Edge AI and Privacy Concerns

Edge AI refers to the deployment of AI models directly on devices such as smartphones, sensors, and cameras, enabling real-time processing without the need for constant internet connectivity. Edge AI is revolutionizing industries like **IoT**, **smart homes**, and **autonomous systems**, but it also presents privacy concerns.

a) Data Privacy and Security

Since **edge devices** often process data locally, they can reduce the need for data to be sent to centralized servers, which in turn can improve privacy. However, this also raises the issue of how sensitive data is handled on the devices themselves.

- **Risk:** Sensitive information, such as **personal health data**, **biometric information**, or **location data**, may be processed on edge devices, which may not have the same security safeguards as centralized data centers.
- **Challenge:** Ensuring that edge devices are adequately secured and that user data is protected from unauthorized access or breaches is critical to maintaining privacy.

Solution:

- **Encryption and Anonymization:** Implement **encryption** and **anonymization** techniques to protect data both in transit and on-device. Secure storage and processing of sensitive information on edge devices can help mitigate privacy risks.

Graphical Representation of Edge AI Privacy Concerns:

[Edge Device (IoT, Smart Device)] --> [Processing Sensitive Data Locally]

| |

[Data Privacy Risks] --> [Unauthorized Data Access or Breaches]

This diagram highlights the privacy risks associated with edge AI, particularly when sensitive data is processed and stored locally on devices without proper security measures.

4. Neuro-Symbolic AI and Ethical Dilemmas

Neuro-symbolic AI combines neural networks' ability to learn from large data sets with symbolic reasoning's ability to perform logical inference. This approach aims to bring together the strengths of **deep learning** and **traditional AI reasoning** for more interpretable, explainable, and generalizable AI systems. However, it raises new ethical questions about how symbolic rules are encoded and how reasoning processes are represented.

a) Transparency and Interpretability

While symbolic AI reasoning offers more transparency than deep learning-based approaches, it still requires the careful design of rules and structures, which can be opaque to non-experts.

- **Risk**: If the symbolic rules are poorly designed or inherently biased, the reasoning process of neuro-symbolic AI can lead to biased, unfair, or discriminatory outcomes.
- **Challenge**: Ensuring the interpretability of both neural and symbolic components within neuro-symbolic systems is crucial for building trust and accountability.

Solution:

- **Clear Documentation and Audits**: Ensure that all symbolic rules and logic used in neuro-symbolic systems are well-documented and auditable to prevent hidden biases and errors.

Conclusion

The **emerging innovations** in AI, such as **generative models**, **reinforcement learning**, **edge AI**, and **neuro-symbolic AI**, offer tremendous potential but also present significant ethical challenges. As AI continues to advance, it is crucial to maintain a focus on **responsible AI** by addressing key ethical concerns such as **privacy**, **security**, **bias**, and **accountability**.

To ensure that these technologies are developed and deployed in a way that benefits society, AI developers must adhere to **ethical guidelines**, implement **bias mitigation strategies**, ensure **data privacy** and **security**, and maintain **transparency** in the development and decision-making processes. By doing so, we can maximize the positive impact of AI innovations while minimizing potential harm and safeguarding fundamental ethical principles.

Emerging innovations should be embraced, but they must be guided by **responsibility**, **ethics**, and a commitment to creating AI that aligns with the values and rights of all individuals.

Appendices

Introduction

The field of **Artificial Intelligence (AI)** is vast and multifaceted, involving a range of techniques and technologies that require practical tools and resources for effective learning and development. To complement the theoretical and conceptual aspects covered in this work, this section provides practical **code examples**, links to **open-source resources**, and **guidelines** for further exploration and implementation of AI concepts. These appendices serve as a reference for individuals looking to experiment with AI and **Large Language Models (LLMs)**, providing real-world examples, relevant libraries, and tools that can be integrated into projects and applications.

This section is divided into two primary parts:

1. **Code Examples** – Practical Python code snippets demonstrating AI concepts.
2. **Resources** – A curated list of external resources, including documentation, libraries, courses, and research papers, to deepen your understanding and facilitate your work with AI.

1. Code Examples

a) Simple Text Generation using GPT-2 with Hugging Face

The following code demonstrates how to generate text using the pre-trained **GPT-2 model** from the **Hugging Face Transformers** library. This code can be extended for various natural language processing (NLP) applications, such as chatbots or creative writing assistants.

```
from transformers import GPT2LMHeadModel, GPT2Tokenizer

# Load the pre-trained model and tokenizer from Hugging Face

model_name = 'gpt2'  # You can use 'gpt2-medium', 'gpt2-large', etc.
```

```
model = GPT2LMHeadModel.from_pretrained(model_name)

tokenizer = GPT2Tokenizer.from_pretrained(model_name)


# Encode a prompt text

input_text = "Artificial Intelligence is the future of"

input_ids = tokenizer.encode(input_text, return_tensors='pt')


# Generate text

output = model.generate(input_ids, max_length=50,
num_return_sequences=1, no_repeat_ngram_size=2)


# Decode the output tokens and print the generated text

generated_text = tokenizer.decode(output[0],
skip_special_tokens=True)

print(generated_text)
```

Explanation:

- This code loads the GPT-2 model and tokenizer from **Hugging Face's library**.
- The input_text is encoded and passed into the model to generate text.
- The model.generate() function generates a continuation of the provided prompt based on GPT-2's training.
- The generated text is decoded and printed.

b) Fine-Tuning a Language Model (BERT) for Sentiment Analysis

In this example, we use the **Hugging Face Transformers** library to fine-tune a **BERT model** on a sentiment analysis task. This code demonstrates how to train the model on a simple dataset.

```
from transformers import BertTokenizer,
BertForSequenceClassification, Trainer, TrainingArguments

from datasets import load_dataset


# Load a pre-trained tokenizer and model

model_name = "bert-base-uncased"

tokenizer = BertTokenizer.from_pretrained(model_name)

model =
BertForSequenceClassification.from_pretrained(model_name,
num_labels=2)


# Load a sentiment analysis dataset

dataset = load_dataset("imdb")


# Tokenize the dataset

def tokenize_function(examples):

    return tokenizer(examples["text"], padding="max_length",
truncation=True)
```

```
train_dataset = dataset["train"].map(tokenize_function,
batched=True)
eval_dataset = dataset["test"].map(tokenize_function, batched=True)

# Define training arguments
training_args = TrainingArguments(
    output_dir="./results",
    evaluation_strategy="epoch",
    learning_rate=2e-5,
    per_device_train_batch_size=16,
    per_device_eval_batch_size=16,
    num_train_epochs=3,
    weight_decay=0.01,
)

# Initialize the Trainer
trainer = Trainer(
    model=model,
    args=training_args,
    train_dataset=train_dataset,
    eval_dataset=eval_dataset,
)
```

```
# Train the model
trainer.train()


# Evaluate the model
trainer.evaluate()
```

Explanation:

- This code uses **BERT** from Hugging Face for **sentiment analysis** on the **IMDB** dataset.
- The dataset is tokenized using the pre-trained BERT tokenizer, and the model is fine-tuned using **Trainer** and **TrainingArguments**.
- The training process is run for **3 epochs**, and the performance is evaluated at the end.

c) Simple Image Captioning using CLIP Model

The following example demonstrates the use of the **CLIP model** (Contrastive Language-Image Pretraining) to generate captions for images. CLIP can understand both images and text and associate them in a unified embedding space.

```
from transformers import CLIPProcessor, CLIPModel
from PIL import Image
import requests


# Load the pre-trained CLIP model and processor
model_name = "openai/clip-vit-base-patch32"
model = CLIPModel.from_pretrained(model_name)
```

```
processor = CLIPProcessor.from_pretrained(model_name)

# Load an image from the web
image_url = "https://example.com/image.jpg"  # Replace with a valid image URL
image = Image.open(requests.get(image_url, stream=True).raw)

# Define a list of possible captions
texts = ["a photo of a cat", "a photo of a dog", "a photo of a car"]

# Process the image and texts
inputs = processor(text=texts, images=image, return_tensors="pt", padding=True)

# Perform inference
outputs = model(**inputs)
logits_per_image = outputs.logits_per_image # this is the similarity score
probs = logits_per_image.softmax(dim=1) # apply softmax to get probabilities

# Get the index of the highest probability
caption_index = probs.argmax()
print(f"The model thinks this image is: '{texts[caption_index]}'")
```

Explanation:

- This code uses the **CLIP model** to compare an image with a list of possible captions and selects the one that best matches the image.
- **CLIP** works by associating both image and text representations in the same embedding space, allowing for zero-shot image classification and captioning.

2. Resources

The following resources are provided for developers, researchers, and practitioners who wish to further their understanding of **Large Language Models (LLMs)**, **AI ethics**, and **multimodal AI**. These resources cover documentation, open-source libraries, datasets, courses, and academic research.

a) Libraries and Frameworks

1. **Hugging Face Transformers**:
   - **Description**: Hugging Face provides an extensive collection of pre-trained models for various NLP tasks, including text generation, sentiment analysis, and question answering.
   - **Link**: Hugging Face Transformers
2. **TensorFlow**:
   - **Description**: An open-source machine learning library developed by Google, TensorFlow is widely used for training deep learning models and has robust support for deploying models in production.
   - **Link**: TensorFlow

3. **PyTorch**:
   - **Description**: PyTorch is another popular machine learning library that provides flexibility and speed for developing and training deep learning models. PyTorch is often preferred for research and development due to its dynamic computation graph.
   - **Link**: PyTorch
4. **OpenAI Gym**:
   - **Description**: OpenAI Gym is a toolkit for developing and comparing reinforcement learning algorithms. It provides environments for training AI agents, which is crucial for experimentation with **RL** and **RLHF**.
   - **Link**: OpenAI Gym
5. **Keras**:
   - **Description**: Keras is a high-level neural networks API, written in Python and capable of running on top of **TensorFlow**, making it easy to build and train deep learning models.
   - **Link**: Keras

b) Datasets for AI Research

1. **The IMDB Dataset (for Sentiment Analysis)**:
   - **Description**: The IMDB dataset contains movie reviews, which can be used to train and evaluate sentiment analysis models.
   - **Link**: IMDB Dataset

2. **COCO Dataset (for Image Captioning)**:
    - **Description**: The **COCO** dataset is widely used for image captioning, object detection, and segmentation. It contains over 300,000 images and their corresponding captions.
    - **Link**: COCO Dataset
3. **LibriSpeech (for Speech Recognition)**:
    - **Description**: LibriSpeech is an open-source dataset used for training and evaluating speech recognition models.
    - **Link**: LibriSpeech

c) Online Courses and Tutorials

1. **Deep Learning Specialization by Andrew Ng (Coursera)**:
    - **Description**: A comprehensive series of courses that cover the fundamentals of deep learning, from neural networks to advanced techniques like sequence models.
    - **Link**: Deep Learning Specialization
2. **Fast.ai – Practical Deep Learning for Coders**:
    - **Description**: An online course that teaches deep learning through hands-on projects using the Fast.ai library, which runs on top of PyTorch.
    - **Link**: Fast.ai
3. **Stanford CS224N: Natural Language Processing with Deep Learning**:
    - **Description**: This course provides an in-depth exploration of modern NLP techniques, including transformers and attention mechanisms.
    - **Link**: Stanford CS224N

d) Academic Papers and Research

1. **Attention is All You Need (Vaswani et al.)**:
    - **Description**: The seminal paper that introduced the Transformer architecture, which has since revolutionized NLP.
    - **Link**: Attention is All You Need
2. **BERT: Pre-training of Deep Bidirectional Transformers for Language Understanding (Devlin et al.)**:
    - **Description**: The paper that introduced **BERT**, a transformer-based model that achieved state-of-the-art results on a variety of NLP tasks.
    - **Link**: BERT Paper
3. **GPT-3: Language Models are Few-Shot Learners (Brown et al.)**:
    - **Description**: This paper introduces **GPT-3**, a large language model that has demonstrated remarkable capabilities in **few-shot learning**.
    - **Link**: GPT-3 Paper

The **Appendices** provide a comprehensive toolkit for individuals looking to deepen their understanding of **AI** and **LLMs**. The **code examples** offer practical implementations of key AI techniques, while the **resources** section includes documentation, datasets, courses, and research papers for further exploration. These tools and materials empower AI practitioners to implement the concepts discussed and explore emerging innovations in the AI field, all while adhering to **ethical principles** and **responsible AI** practices.

Glossary

Understanding the terminology used in AI research, development, and deployment is crucial for navigating this complex and fast-evolving field. This glossary serves as a helpful reference for both newcomers and experienced practitioners.

A

- **Activation Function**: A mathematical function applied to the output of a neuron in a neural network to introduce non-linearity into the model, enabling it to learn complex patterns.
- **Adversarial Attack**: A type of input manipulation aimed at misleading an AI model. These inputs are designed to exploit the vulnerabilities of the model and make it perform incorrectly.
- **AI Ethics**: The branch of ethics that studies the moral implications of AI technology. It addresses issues such as **bias, privacy, accountability**, and the **impact of AI** on society.
- **Autoencoder**: A type of neural network used to learn efficient representations of data, typically for dimensionality reduction or feature learning. It consists of an encoder and a decoder.

B

- **Backpropagation**: A key algorithm for training neural networks, where the model's error is propagated backward through the network to adjust the weights of the neurons and minimize the loss.

- **Bias (in Machine Learning)**: A systematic error introduced by an AI model due to assumptions made during training. In a broader sense, bias can also refer to prejudices in data that lead to unfair or discriminatory outputs.
- **Batch Learning**: A type of machine learning where the model is trained on the entire dataset at once, as opposed to online learning, where data is processed incrementally.
- **Bias-Variance Tradeoff**: The balance between bias and variance in machine learning models. High bias leads to underfitting, while high variance leads to overfitting. The goal is to find a model with low bias and low variance.

C

- **Classification**: A supervised learning task where the goal is to assign input data to one of several predefined categories. For example, classifying emails as "spam" or "not spam."
- **Clustering**: An unsupervised learning task that involves grouping similar data points together based on their features. The goal is to identify inherent structures or patterns in the data.
- **Computer Vision**: A subfield of AI that focuses on enabling machines to interpret and understand visual information from the world, such as images and videos.
- **Convolutional Neural Network (CNN)**: A type of deep neural network primarily used for processing and analyzing visual data, such as images. CNNs are designed to automatically learn spatial hierarchies of features from images.

D

- **Data Augmentation**: The process of artificially increasing the size of a training dataset by creating modified versions of existing data. This is often done in image processing by rotating, flipping, or scaling images.
- **Deep Learning**: A subset of machine learning that uses multi-layered neural networks to model complex patterns and representations in large datasets. It is especially effective in tasks like image recognition, speech processing, and natural language processing.
- **Deep Reinforcement Learning (DRL)**: A type of reinforcement learning where deep learning models (such as CNNs or LSTMs) are used to handle high-dimensional input spaces, like images or text, for decision-making.

E

- **Epoch**: One complete pass through the entire training dataset during the training of a machine learning model. Multiple epochs are typically required to train a model effectively.
- **Explainable AI (XAI)**: A field of AI focused on creating models whose decisions can be easily understood by humans. This is important for accountability, transparency, and trust in AI systems.
- **Encoder-Decoder Model**: A type of model architecture used in sequence-to-sequence tasks, such as machine translation. The encoder processes the input sequence, while the decoder generates the output sequence.

F

- **Feature Engineering**: The process of selecting, modifying, or creating new input variables (features) from raw data to improve the performance of a machine learning model.
- **Fine-Tuning**: The process of taking a pre-trained model and adapting it to a specific task by training it on a smaller dataset. Fine-tuning allows the model to learn domain-specific patterns while leveraging the general knowledge acquired from the larger dataset.
- **Fully Connected Layer**: A layer in a neural network where each neuron is connected to every neuron in the previous layer. Fully connected layers are used to aggregate information across features and make predictions.

G

- **Generative Model**: A type of model that learns to generate new data that resembles the training data. Examples include **Generative Adversarial Networks (GANs)** and **variational autoencoders (VAEs)**.
- **Gradient Descent**: A common optimization algorithm used to minimize the loss function in machine learning by iteratively adjusting model parameters in the direction of the steepest decrease in the loss.
- **GAN (Generative Adversarial Network)**: A type of generative model composed of two networks: a generator, which creates synthetic data, and a discriminator, which attempts to distinguish between real and fake data.

H

- **Hyperparameter**: A parameter that is set before the model training process begins. Hyperparameters control aspects like the learning rate, batch size, and the number of hidden layers in a neural network.
- **Human-in-the-Loop (HITL)**: A model training approach that involves human intervention during the decision-making or learning process. This is often used to incorporate human judgment and feedback into AI systems.

I

- **Intelligent Agent**: An entity in AI that perceives its environment, makes decisions, and takes actions to achieve specific goals. Intelligent agents are central to fields such as robotics and autonomous systems.
- **Interpretability**: The ability of a machine learning model to provide explanations for its predictions. It is closely related to **explainable AI** and is crucial for ensuring that AI systems can be trusted and understood by humans.
- **Inference**: The process of using a trained machine learning model to make predictions or decisions based on new, unseen data.

J

- **Joint Embedding**: A technique in machine learning where two or more data modalities (such as images and text) are embedded into a shared vector space, allowing them to be compared or used together.

K

- **Knowledge Graph**: A structured representation of knowledge that connects entities (e.g., people, places, things) and their relationships. Knowledge graphs are often used in AI for tasks like search, recommendation, and question answering.
- **K-Means Clustering**: An unsupervised learning algorithm that partitions data into a predefined number of clusters by minimizing the variance within each cluster.

L

- **Latent Variables**: Variables that are not directly observed but are inferred from the data. In probabilistic models, latent variables are used to model underlying structures or patterns in the data.
- **Long Short-Term Memory (LSTM)**: A type of recurrent neural network (RNN) designed to model long-term dependencies in sequential data, such as time-series data or natural language.

M

- **Model Evaluation**: The process of assessing the performance of a machine learning model using various metrics, such as **accuracy**, **precision**, **recall**, and **F1 score**.
- **Multimodal AI**: AI systems that can process and integrate information from multiple modalities (e.g., text, image, audio) to improve understanding and performance on complex tasks.

N

- **Natural Language Processing (NLP)**: A branch of AI that focuses on the interaction between computers and human language. NLP tasks include **text classification**, **machine translation**, **sentiment analysis**, and **question answering**.
- **Neural Network**: A computational model inspired by the structure of the human brain, consisting of layers of interconnected neurons that can learn to perform tasks through training.
- **Neuro-Symbolic AI**: A hybrid approach combining the learning capabilities of neural networks with symbolic reasoning techniques. This approach aims to combine the strengths of both methods to improve generalization and reasoning.

O

- **Overfitting**: A scenario in which a machine learning model learns the training data too well, capturing noise and fluctuations that do not generalize to new data. Overfitting typically occurs when the model is too complex for the dataset.

P

- **Perceptron**: A type of neural network model consisting of a single layer of neurons. It is a foundational building block for modern neural networks and deep learning.
- **Precision**: A performance metric that measures the proportion of true positive predictions out of all positive predictions made by a model.

- **Recall**: A performance metric that measures the proportion of true positive predictions out of all actual positive instances in the data.
- **Privacy-Preserving AI**: AI techniques designed to protect user privacy, such as **differential privacy**, which ensures that individual data points cannot be inferred from the model's output.

Q

- **Q-Learning**: A type of reinforcement learning algorithm where an agent learns the value of actions based on a reward signal, allowing it to make decisions that maximize cumulative rewards.

R

- **Reinforcement Learning (RL)**: A type of machine learning where an agent learns to make decisions by interacting with an environment and receiving rewards or penalties based on its actions.
- **Recurrent Neural Network (RNN)**: A type of neural network designed for sequential data, where the output of one step is fed back into the network as input for the next step.

S

- **Supervised Learning**: A type of machine learning where the model is trained on labeled data, meaning that both the input and the correct output are provided to the model during training.

- **Self-Supervised Learning**: A machine learning technique where a model learns from data that has been automatically labeled through pre-defined structures or transformations, without explicit human labeling.

T

- **TensorFlow**: An open-source machine learning library developed by Google for building and training deep learning models. It is widely used for developing AI applications in various fields.
- **Transformers**: A type of deep learning model architecture that uses self-attention mechanisms to handle sequential data more efficiently than traditional recurrent models. Transformers have become the foundation for models like BERT and GPT.

U

- **Unsupervised Learning**: A type of machine learning where the model is trained on data without explicit labels. The goal is to identify patterns or structures in the data, such as clustering or dimensionality reduction.

V

- **Variational Autoencoder (VAE)**: A type of generative model used for tasks like image generation and anomaly detection. VAEs learn probabilistic distributions over the data and can generate new data points similar to the training data.

W

- **Weights**: Parameters in a neural network that determine the strength of connections between neurons. During training, these weights are adjusted to minimize the loss function and improve the model's performance.

X

- **XAI (Explainable AI)**: A field of AI focused on creating models that can explain their reasoning and decision-making process in ways that humans can understand.

Y

- **YAML (YAML Ain't Markup Language)**: A human-readable data serialization standard used to define configurations for machine learning models, pipelines, or data processing tasks.

Z

- **Zero-shot Learning**: A machine learning paradigm where a model is capable of correctly performing tasks without having been explicitly trained on examples from the task. The model leverages knowledge from other tasks or modalities.

This glossary serves as a guide to understanding the key terms and concepts in the rapidly evolving field of AI. Whether you're just beginning your journey in AI or are an experienced practitioner, having a solid understanding of these terms will enhance your ability to navigate and contribute to AI research, development, and ethical discussions.

Bibliography

Introduction

The **bibliography** is a vital component of any academic work, providing proper attribution to sources that influenced the ideas, research, and conclusions within the text. For books and articles discussing **Artificial Intelligence (AI)**, **Machine Learning (ML)**, **Natural Language Processing (NLP)**, and **Ethical AI** principles, it is important to cite authoritative texts that provide foundational knowledge, current research, and practical frameworks in these fields.

1. Key Texts in Artificial Intelligence and Machine Learning

a) **Goodfellow, I., Bengio, Y., & Courville, A. (2016).** *Deep learning.* MIT Press.

- This seminal work provides an in-depth exploration of deep learning techniques, the foundation of modern AI and neural networks. It covers theory, algorithms, and applications across a wide range of domains in AI.

b) **Russell, S., & Norvig, P. (2020).** *Artificial Intelligence: A modern approach* (4th ed.). Pearson.

- One of the most comprehensive and widely used textbooks on AI. It provides a thorough introduction to the fundamentals of AI, including search algorithms, logic, decision-making, learning, and problem-solving.

c) **Bishop, C. M. (2006).** *Pattern recognition and machine learning.* Springer.

- A key reference for understanding statistical pattern recognition techniques and their applications in machine learning, including graphical models, decision theory, and optimization.

d) **Mitchell, T. M. (1997).** *Machine learning.* McGraw-Hill.

- This text provides foundational knowledge in machine learning, covering supervised and unsupervised learning, reinforcement learning, and the theory behind various ML algorithms.

---

2. Essential Resources in Natural Language Processing (NLP)

a) **Jurafsky, D., & Martin, J. H. (2020).** *Speech and language processing* (3rd ed.). Pearson.

- This textbook is a comprehensive guide to NLP, including detailed discussions on syntax, semantics, parsing, machine translation, and deep learning applications in language processing.

b) **Vaswani, A., Shazeer, N., Parmar, N., Uszkoreit, J., Jones, L., Gomez, A. N., Kaiser, Ł., & Polosukhin, I. (2017).** Attention is all you need. *Proceedings of NeurIPS 2017.*

- This landmark paper introduced the **transformer model**, which has become the foundation for recent advances in NLP, including models like **BERT**, **GPT**, and **T5**.

c) **Devlin, J., Chang, M. W., Lee, K., & Toutanova, K. (2018).** BERT: Pre-training of deep bidirectional transformers for language understanding. *Proceedings of NAACL-HLT 2019.*

- This paper introduced **BERT**, a deep transformer model that achieved state-of-the-art results in multiple NLP tasks. It provides the basis for many modern NLP models.

d) **Hirschberg, J., & Manning, C. D. (2015).** Advances in natural language processing. *Science*, 349(6245), 273-278. https://doi.org/10.1126/science.aab0619

- This paper reviews the advancements in NLP, providing insights into the growth of AI techniques that can understand and generate natural language.

---

3. Ethical AI and Responsible AI Practices

a) **Binns, R. (2018).** *On the ethical implications of AI and machine learning systems.* ACM SIGAI Artificial Intelligence, 2(4), 27-33.

- This article discusses the ethical challenges posed by AI systems, including bias, accountability, and the societal impacts of automation.

b) **O'Neil, C. (2016).** *Weapons of math destruction: How big data increases inequality and threatens democracy.* Crown Publishing Group.

- A critical examination of the ethical implications of AI and big data, particularly how algorithms perpetuate social inequalities and power imbalances.

c) **Jobin, A., Ienca, M., & Vayena, E. (2019).** The global landscape of AI ethics guidelines. *Nature Machine Intelligence*, 1(9), 389-399. https://doi.org/10.1038/s42256-019-0088-2

- This paper provides an overview of global AI ethics guidelines and the challenges faced by policymakers, developers, and companies in ensuring ethical AI development.

d) **Mittelstadt, B. D., Allo, P., Taddeo, M., Wachter, S., & Floridi, L. (2016).** The ethics of algorithms: Mapping the debate. *Big Data & Society*, 3(2), 1-21. https://doi.org/10.1177/2053951716679679

- A critical analysis of the ethical considerations surrounding algorithmic decision-making, exploring issues like fairness, transparency, and accountability.

4. Emerging Innovations in AI

a) **Silver, D., Hubert, T., Schrittwieser, J., Antonoglou, I., Lai, M., & Lanctot, M. (2017).** Mastering the game of Go without human knowledge. *Nature*, 550(7676), 354-359. https://doi.org/10.1038/nature24270

- This landmark paper discusses the development of **AlphaGo**, an AI that achieved superhuman performance in the game of Go through reinforcement learning and deep neural networks.

b) **LeCun, Y., Bengio, Y., & Hinton, G. (2015).** Deep learning. *Nature*, 521(7553), 436-444. https://doi.org/10.1038/nature14539

- A foundational paper in deep learning, where the authors explain the rise of deep neural networks and their transformative impact on AI applications.

c) **Schulman, J., Moritz, P., Leike, J., Ziegler, D., Sutskever, I., & Abbeel, P. (2015).** High-dimensional continuous control using generalized advantage estimation. *Proceedings of NeurIPS 2015.*

- This paper introduces **Generalized Advantage Estimation (GAE)**, a technique used in reinforcement learning to improve training efficiency and performance.

d) **Vaswani, A., Shazeer, N., Parmar, N., Uszkoreit, J., Jones, L., Gomez, A. N., Kaiser, Ł., & Polosukhin, I. (2017).** Attention is all you need. *Proceedings of NeurIPS 2017.*

- The paper that introduced **Transformers**, which revolutionized NLP and has since become the core architecture for many large-scale language models.

e) **Krizhevsky, A., Sutskever, I., & Hinton, G. E. (2012).** ImageNet classification with deep convolutional neural networks. *Advances in Neural Information Processing Systems*, 25, 1097-1105.

- This paper introduced **AlexNet**, a deep convolutional neural network that won the ImageNet competition in 2012 and sparked widespread adoption of deep learning for image classification.

5. Resources for Further Learning and Research

a) Online Courses

1. **Deep Learning Specialization by Andrew Ng (Coursera)**:
   - A comprehensive series of courses that cover the fundamental concepts of deep learning, from basic neural networks to advanced topics such as CNNs, RNNs, and reinforcement learning.
   - **Link**: Deep Learning Specialization
2. **Stanford CS224N: Natural Language Processing with Deep Learning (Stanford University)**:
   - An advanced course that covers deep learning models for NLP, including transformers, BERT, and GPT models.
   - **Link**: CS224N Course
3. **Fast.ai – Practical Deep Learning for Coders**:
   - A hands-on deep learning course focused on practical implementations using the **Fast.ai** library, which runs on top of **PyTorch**.
   - **Link**: Fast.ai Course

b) Open-Source Libraries and Tools

1. **Hugging Face Transformers**:
   - A leading library for working with **transformers**, offering a wide range of pre-trained models for NLP tasks such as text generation, classification, and question answering.
   - **Link**: Hugging Face Transformers
2. **TensorFlow**:
   - A popular open-source framework for machine learning and deep learning, widely used for building AI models and deploying them at scale.
   - **Link**: TensorFlow
3. **PyTorch**:
   - A flexible deep learning framework that has gained popularity for research and development due to its dynamic computation graph and ease of use.
   - **Link**: PyTorch

c) Academic Journals and Databases

1. **IEEE Transactions on Neural Networks and Learning Systems**:
   - A premier journal for research in machine learning, neural networks, and deep learning, including both theoretical and applied papers.
   - **Link**: IEEE Transactions

2. **arXiv.org**:
    - A free repository for academic papers across various fields, including AI and machine learning. Many foundational AI papers are published on arXiv before being formally peer-reviewed.
    - **Link**: arXiv

Conclusion

The **Bibliography** section serves as a valuable resource for anyone seeking to expand their knowledge of **AI**, **machine learning**, and **ethical considerations in AI**. By exploring the books, articles, research papers, online courses, and open-source tools listed here, readers can deepen their understanding of the topics discussed in this book and stay up to date with the latest advancements in the field.

www.ingramcontent.com/pod-product-compliance
Lightning Source LLC
LaVergne TN
LVHW050302210926
848481LV00014BA/371